SPOTLIGHT

MYRTLE BEACH

JIM MOREKIS

Contents

MYRTLE BEACH

MYRTLE BEACH AND THE GRAND STRAND

The West has Las Vegas, Florida has Orlando, and South Carolina has Myrtle Beach. There's no Bellagio Resort or Magic Kingdom here, but Myrtle Beach remains the number one travel destination in the state, with even more visitors than Charleston. Unlike Charleston, you'll find little history here. With several theme parks, 100 golf courses, 50 miniature golf courses, over 2,000 restaurants—not to mention miles of beautiful shoreline—Myrtle Beach is built for all-out vacation enjoyment.

The hot, hazy height of the summer also marks the busy season on the Strand. Its long main drag, Kings Highway (a.k.a. Business U.S. 17), is packed full of families on the go eager for more swimming, more shopping, more eating, and just plain more.

While to many people the name Myrtle Beach conjures an image of tacky, downscale people doing tacky, downscale things, that's an outmoded stereotype. Tacky is certainly still in vogue here, but an influx of higher-quality development, both in accommodations and entertainment value, has lifted the bar significantly. Rather than slumming in a beat-up motel, quaffing PBR on the beach, and loading up on $2 T-shirts like in the "good old days," a typical Myrtle Beach vacation now involves a stay in a large condo apartment with flat-screen TVs, a full kitchen, and a sumptuous palmetto-lined

HIGHLIGHTS

NORTH CAROLINA

SOUTH CAROLINA

Ocean Drive Beach
Barefoot Landing
Carolina Opry
Broadway at the Beach
Myrtle Beach
Brookgreen Gardens
Huntington Beach State Park
Georgetown
Hampton Plantation

ATLANTIC OCEAN

0   10 mi
0   10 km

© AVALON TRAVEL

LOOK FOR ◖ TO FIND RECOMMENDED SIGHTS, ACTIVITIES, DINING, AND LODGING.

◖ **Broadway at the Beach:** You'll find good cheesy fun along with tons of interesting shops, theme restaurants, and, of course, miniature golf (page 12).

◖ **Barefoot Landing:** North Myrtle Beach's answer to Broadway at the Beach, with the Alabama Theatre and the House of Blues nearby (page 15).

◖ **Ocean Drive Beach:** The still-beating, still-shuffling heart of the Grand Strand is also the center of shag dancing culture (page 17).

◖ **Carolina Opry:** This popular show offers corny but quality family entertainment in an intimate, friendly setting (page 20).

◖ **Brookgreen Gardens:** Enjoy the country's largest collection of outdoor sculptures, set amid a fine collection of formal gardens (page 43).

◖ **Huntington Beach State Park:** The scenic beach combines with one-of-a-kind Atalaya Castle to make for a unique getaway (page 44).

◖ **Hampton Plantation:** This historic Georgian mansion on the scenic Wambaw Creek inspired a South Carolina poet laureate to give it to the state for posterity (page 54).

pool; dining at the House of Blues; having drinks at the Hard Rock Café; stops at high-profile attractions like Ripley's Aquarium; and shopping at trendy retailers like Anthropologie and Abercrombie & Fitch.

The Grand Strand on which Myrtle Beach sits—a long, sandy peninsula stretching 60 miles from Winyah Bay to the North Carolina border—has also been a vacation playground for generations of South Carolinians. Unlike Hilton Head, where New York and Midwestern accents are more common than Lowcountry drawls, Myrtle Beach and the Grand Strand remain largely homegrown passions, with many visitors living within a few hours' drive. Despite

the steady increase of money and high-dollar development in the area, its strongly regional nature works to your advantage in that prices are generally lower than in Vegas or Orlando.

To the south of Myrtle proper lies the understated, affluent, and relaxing Pawleys Island, with nearby Murrells Inlet and its great seafood restaurants. Unique, eclectic Brookgreen Gardens hosts the largest collection of outdoor sculpture in the country, with one-of-a-kind Huntington Beach State Park literally right across the street.

Even farther south, in the northern quarter of the Lowcountry proper, you'll find a totally different scene: the remnants of the Carolina rice culture in quaint old Georgetown, and the

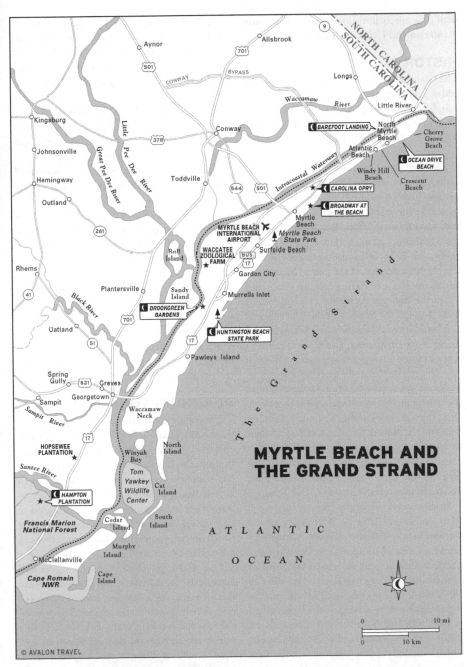

MYRTLE BEACH AND THE GRAND STRAND

NORTH CAROLINA
SOUTH CAROLINA

Aynor
Allsbrook
Longs
Little River
Kingsburg
Conway
BAREFOOT LANDING
North Myrtle Beach
Cherry Grove Beach
Johnsonville
Atlantic Beach
OCEAN DRIVE BEACH
Windy Hill Beach
Crescent Beach
Hemingway
Toddville
CAROLINA OPRY
Outland
BROADWAY AT THE BEACH
MYRTLE BEACH INTERNATIONAL AIRPORT
Myrtle Beach
Myrtle Beach State Park
WACCATEE ZOOLOGICAL FARM
Surfside Beach
Rhems
Bull Island
Garden City
Planterville
Sandy Island
Murrells Inlet
BROOKGREEN GARDENS
Oatland
HUNTINGTON BEACH STATE PARK
Pawleys Island
Spring Gully
Graves
Georgetown
Waccamaw Neck
Sampit
HOPSEWEE PLANTATION
Winyah Bay
North Island
Santee River
Tom Yawkey Wildlife Center
Cat Island
HAMPTON PLANTATION
Francis Marion National Forest
Cedar Island
South Island
McClellanville
Murphy Island
Cape Romain NWR
Cape Island

ATLANTIC

OCEAN

The Grand Strand

MYRTLE BEACH AND
THE GRAND STRAND

0   10 mi
0   10 km

© AVALON TRAVEL

haunting antebellum mansions at Hampton Plantation and Hopsewee Plantation.

HISTORY

The Grand Strand was once the happy hunting and shellfish-gathering grounds of the Waccamaw people, whose legacy is still felt today in the name of the dominant river in the region and the Strand's main drag itself, Kings Highway, which is actually built on an old Native American trail.

The southern portion of the Strand, especially Georgetown and Pawleys Island, rapidly became home to a number of rice plantations soon after the area was colonized. However, the area now known as Myrtle Beach didn't share in the wealth since its soil and topography weren't conducive to the plantation system. Indeed, the northern portion of the Grand Strand was largely uninhabited during colonial times, and hurricane damage prevented much development through the first half of the 19th century.

That changed after the Civil War with the boom of nearby Conway to the west, now the seat of Horry County (pronounced "OR-ee"). As Conway's lumber and export economy grew, a railroad spur was built to bring in lumber from the coast, much of which was owned by a single firm, the Conway Lumber Company. Lumber company employees began using the rail lines to take vacation time on the Strand, in effect becoming the first of millions of tourists to the area. At this time it was simply called "New Town," in contrast to Conway's "Old Town."

In the second half of the 19th century, Civil War veteran Franklin G. Burroughs, of the Burroughs and Collins Company, which supplied lumber and turpentine to Conway business interests, sought to expand the tourism profitability of the coastal area. He died in 1897, but his heirs continued his dream, inaugurated by the opening of the Seaside Inn in 1901. The first bona fide resort came in the 1920s with the building of the Arcady resort, which included the first golf course in the area.

In 1938 Burroughs's widow, Adeline, known locally as "Miss Addie," was credited with giving the town its modern name, after the locally abundant wax myrtle shrub. During this time, locals on the Strand originated the shagging subculture, built around the dance of the same name and celebrated at numerous pavilions and "beach clubs." The building of Myrtle Beach Air Force Base in 1940—now closed—brought further growth and jobs to the area.

Tourism, especially, grew apace here until Hurricane Hazel virtually wiped the slate clean in 1954. In typical Carolinian fashion, residents and landowners made lemonade out of lemons, using the hurricane's devastation as an excuse to build even bigger resort developments, including a plethora of golf courses.

Since then, the Strand has grown to encompass about 250,000 permanent residents, with about 10 million visitors on top of that each year. A huge influx of money in the 1990s led to a higher-dollar form of development on the coast, sadly leading to the demolition of many of the old beach pavilions in favor of new attractions and massive condo high-rises.

PLANNING YOUR TIME

The most important thing to remember is that the Grand Strand is *long*—60 miles from one end to the other. This has real-world effects that need to be taken into account. For example, while the separate municipality of North Myrtle Beach (actually a fairly recent aggregation of several small beachside communities) may sound like it is right next door to Myrtle Beach proper, getting from one to the other can take half an hour even in light traffic.

Due to this geographical stretching, as well as to all the attractions, it is impossible to cover this area in a single day, and even two days is a ridiculously short amount of time. That's probably the main reason many folks indulge in a weekly rental. Not only does it give you enough time to see everything, it enables you to relax, slow down, and enjoy the beaches and the general laid-back attitude.

In May, Memorial Day weekend and Bike Week have traditionally signaled the beginning of the tourism season in Myrtle Beach. The busy season exactly corresponds with the hottest months of the year, July and August. This is when crowds are at their peak, restaurants are most crowded, and the two spurs of U.S. 17 are at their most gridlocked.

Springtime in Myrtle Beach is quite nice, but keep in mind that water temperatures are still chilly through April. There is almost always one last cold snap in March that augurs the spring.

Personally, I recommend hitting Myrtle Beach just as the busy season wanes, right after Labor Day. Rooms are significantly cheaper, but most everything is still fully open and adequately staffed, with the added benefit of the biggest crush of visitors being absent.

Winter on the Grand Strand is very slow, as befitting this very seasonal locale. Many restaurants, especially down the Strand near Murrells Inlet, close entirely through February.

ORIENTATION

Don't get too hung up on place names around here. This part of the Strand comprises several different municipalities, from Surfside Beach to the south up to Little River near the North Carolina border, but for all intents and purposes it's one big place all its own. As a general rule,

development (read: money) is moving more quickly to the North Myrtle Beach area rather than the older Myrtle Beach proper to the south.

North Myrtle is actually a recent aggregation of several historic beachfront communities: Windy Hill, Crescent Beach, Cherry Grove, and Ocean Drive. You'll see numerous signs announcing the entrance or exit into or out of these communities, but keep in mind you're still technically in North Myrtle Beach.

The Grand Strand grid is based on a system of east-west avenues beginning just north of Myrtle Beach State Park. Confusingly, these are separated into "North" and "South" avenues. Perhaps even more confusing, North Myrtle Beach also uses its own distinct north-and-south avenue system, also for roads running east-west. Got it? It goes like this: Myrtle Beach starts with 29th Avenue South at the Myrtle Beach International Airport and goes up to 1st Avenue South just past Family Kingdom Amusement Park. From here, the avenues are labeled as "North" from 1st Avenue North up to 82nd Avenue North, which concludes Myrtle Beach proper. North Myrtle Beach begins at 48th Avenue South near Barefoot Landing and goes up to Main Street (the center of the shag culture). It continues with 1st Avenue North, goes up to 24th Avenue North (Cherry Grove Beach), and finally concludes at 61st Avenue North, near the North Carolina state line.

Sights

◖ BROADWAY AT THE BEACH

Love it or hate it, Broadway at the Beach (1325 Celebrity Circle, 800/386-4662, www.broadwayatthebeach.com, summer daily 10 A.M.-11 P.M., winter daily 11 A.M.-6 P.M.), between 21st and 29th Avenues, is one of Myrtle's biggest and flashiest attractions—which is saying a lot. First opened over 15 years ago and added onto significantly since then, this collection of three hotels, over two dozen restaurants, about 50 shops, and a dozen kid-oriented activities sprawls over 350 acres with several other major attractions, restaurants, and clubs (such as the Hard Rock Café and Planet Hollywood) on its periphery.

Just like the Magic Kingdom that many of Myrtle's attractions seek to emulate, Broadway at the Beach has at its center a large lagoon, around which everything else is situated. Needless to say there's also a massive parking lot. Activity goes on all day and well into the wee hours, with the weekly Tuesday-night fireworks a big draw. While there's plenty to do, what with the great shops, tasty treats, and fun piped-in music following you everywhere, it's also fun just to walk around.

The main complaint about Broadway at the Beach has to do with the price of the various attractions within the park, some of which are fairly small-scale. Indeed, the quality of the attractions within Broadway at the Beach varies, and much depends on what floats your boat, but you can still find plenty to enjoy as long as you know the scoop ahead of time. Here's a quick guide to the specific attractions.

The biggest new attraction at Broadway—and it's really big—is **Wonderworks** (1313 Celebrity Circle, 843/626-9962, www.wonderworksonline.com, $23 adults, $15 children). You can't miss it—look for the thing that looks exactly like a massive, life-size, crumbling, upside-down creepy mansion. Inside you'll find a wide and quite varied assortment of interactive experiences designed to let you know what it's like to be upside down, or on a bed of nails, or in a hurricane, or freezing after the *Titanic* sank, and things of that nature. Think Ripley's Believe It or Not updated for a modern age, complete with laser tag.

Harry Potter fans will likely enjoy **MagiQuest** (1185 Celebrity Circle, 843/913-9460, www.magiquest.com, $26-40), which takes you on a 90-minute journey to find clues that lead to hidden treasure. Folks of an older generation will find it a surprisingly high-tech experience for something dealing with the ancient arts of wizardry—including an orientation session and the programmable wands that are indispensable to the quest. But don't worry; the young ones will get it.

MagiQuest has a certain addictive quality, and many people opt to go back for more (additional quests cost less) after their usually confusing, full-price first experience. Note that there's an intro game you can play online, which might help you get acquainted. Like many attractions at Myrtle Beach, this one can get very crowded, which is certain to impede the quality of your experience (Whose wand uncovered the clue? Who knows?). Try to go right when it opens.

Similarly medieval—and right nearby—is **Medieval Times** (2904 Fantasy Way, 843/236-4635, www.medievaltimes.com, $51 adults, $31 ages 3-12), a combination dinner theater and medieval tournament reenactment.

Now that almost all of the old-fashioned amusement parks at Myrtle Beach are gone, victims of "modernization," you can find a facsimile of sorts at **Pavilion Nostalgia Park** (843/913-9400, www.pavilionnostalgiapark.com, summer daily 11 A.M.-11 P.M., hours vary in other seasons, rides $4 each), which seeks to simulate the days of Myrtle gone by.

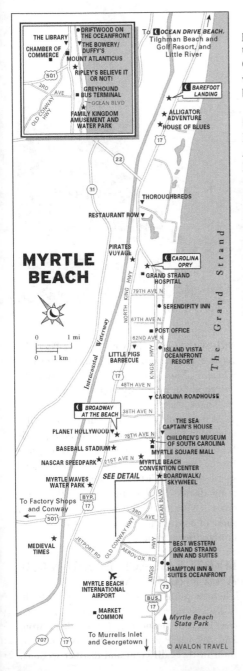

THE LIBRARY
CHAMBER OF COMMERCE
● DRIFTWOOD ON THE OCEANFRONT
▼ THE BOWERY/ DUFFY'S
MOUNT ATLANTICUS
RIPLEY'S BELIEVE IT OR NOT!
GREYHOUND ■ BUS TERMINAL
OCEAN BLVD
FAMILY KINGDOM AMUSEMENT AND WATER PARK
To 【 OCEAN DRIVE BEACH, Tilghman Beach and Golf Resort, and Little River
【 BAREFOOT LANDING
★ ALLIGATOR ADVENTURE
★ HOUSE OF BLUES
THOROUGHBREDS
RESTAURANT ROW ▼
PIRATES VOYAGE ★
【 CAROLINA OPRY
■ GRAND STRAND HOSPITAL
● SERENDIPITY INN
● POST OFFICE
● ISLAND VISTA OCEANFRONT RESORT
LITTLE PIGS BARBECUE
▼ CAROLINA ROADHOUSE
【 BROADWAY AT THE BEACH
THE SEA CAPTAIN'S HOUSE
PLANET HOLLYWOOD ▼
CHILDREN'S MUSEUM OF SOUTH CAROLINA
BASEBALL STADIUM ★
MYRTLE SQUARE MALL
NASCAR SPEEDPARK ★
MYRTLE BEACH CONVENTION CENTER
MYRTLE WAVES WATER PARK ★
SEE DETAIL
★ BOARDWALK/ SKYWHEEL
To Factory Shops and Conway
MEDIEVAL TIMES
BEST WESTERN GRAND STRAND INN AND SUITES
HAMPTON INN & SUITES OCEANFRONT
MYRTLE BEACH INTERNATIONAL AIRPORT
■ MARKET COMMON
Myrtle Beach State Park
To Murrells Inlet and Georgetown
© AVALON TRAVEL

MYRTLE BEACH

0   1 mi
0   1 km

Intracoastal Waterway

North King Hwy

Kings Hwy

The Grand Strand

Of course nowhere in Myrtle is really complete without miniature golf, and Broadway at the Beach's version is **Dragon's Lair Fantasy Golf** (1197 Celebrity Circle, 843/913-9301, $9), with two medieval-themed 18-hole courses boasting a fire-breathing dragon.

Ripley's Aquarium

If you've been to Boston's New England Aquarium, don't expect something similar at Ripley's Aquarium (1110 Celebrity Circle, 800/734-8888, www.ripleysaquarium.com, Sun.-Thurs. 9 A.M.-8 P.M., Fri.-Sat. 9 A.M.-9 P.M., $22 adults, $11 ages 6-11, $4 ages 2-5, free under age 2) at Broadway at the Beach. This is a smaller but quite delightful aquarium built primarily for entertainment purposes rather than education. Calming music plays throughout, and a moving sidewalk takes you around and under a huge main tank filled with various marine creatures. There's even the requisite stingray-petting touch tank.

You'll no doubt see the garish billboards for the Aquarium up and down U.S. 17, featuring massive sharks baring rows of scary teeth. But don't expect an over-the-top shark exhibit—the truth is that most of the sharks in the aquarium are smaller and much more peaceful.

NASCAR SpeedPark

Just outside Broadway at the Beach you'll find the NASCAR SpeedPark (1820 21st Ave. N., 843/918-8725, www.nascarspeedpark.com, summer daily 10 A.M.-11 P.M., shorter hours in other seasons, from $30), where can you speed around at 50 mph in a fairly decent replica of an actual NASCAR track. Because there are several different tracks to choose from, based on age and difficulty, there's something here for adults and kids alike.

The serious track, Thunder Road, is open only to drivers age 16 and over; it allows drivers to get into half-size versions of Nextel Cup cars. Pint-size drivers 48, 40, and 36 inches

© JIM MOREKIS

Ripley's Aquarium

tall can take part in racing on the Champions, Qualifier, and Kiddie Speedway courses, respectively. As if all that's not enough, there are water-based racing courses and, this being Myrtle Beach, NASCAR-themed miniature golf.

If you're worried about metal-shearing, flame-spewing, multiple-car pileups like in a real NASCAR race, don't. Safety is a paramount concern at this national chain of parks, and the likelihood of an accident at the SpeedPark is far less than on crowded U.S. 17, a stone's throw away.

Myrtle Waves Water Park

Billed as South Carolina's largest water park, Myrtle Waves Water Park (U.S. 17 Bypass and 10th Ave. N., 843/913-9260, www.myrtle-waves.com, summer daily 10 A.M.-6 P.M., hours vary in other seasons, $28 age 7 and over, $22 ages 3-6, free under age 3) is right across the street from Broadway at the Beach, covers 20 acres, and features all kinds of safe fun "rides,"

such as the Ocean in Motion Wave Pool, the Layzee River, and the Saturation Station, wherein a huge water volcano absolutely soaks everybody in proximity every five minutes or so. That's just to name a few.

As you would expect, there are plenty of lifeguards on hand at all the rides. Food is plentiful if unremarkable, and there are shaded areas for the less adventurous to chill while the kids splash around. With one admission price covering all rides all day, this is one of the better deals in Myrtle Beach, which has more than its share of confusingly (and occasionally exorbitantly) priced attractions.

MYRTLE BEACH BOARDWALK AND PROMENADE

The new pride of old Myrtle, the Boardwalk (www.visitmyrtlebeach.com, daily 24 hours, free) is a fun, meandering 1.2-mile jaunt from 2nd Avenue Pier to the 14th Avenue Pier. Built in three different and distinct sections, the point of the Boardwalk is not only to take you through the more commercial areas of the beachfront area but to provide easy pedestrian beach access. One section provides a nice peaceful walking experience amid the dune-scape.

Unveiled in 2010, the Boardwalk has been a very important civic and morale improvement in the wake of the loss of the old pavilion nearby, now mostly a grassy field.

Skywheel

You can't miss spotting the new Skywheel (1110 N. Ocean Blvd., 843/839-9200, myrtlebeachskywheel.com, summer daily noon–midnight, $13 adults, $9 children), a huge Ferris wheel dominating the skyline at the new Boardwalk. The cars are family-size, fully enclosed, and offer a great view of the ocean and surrounding area during the approximately 10-minute, three-rotation trip.

the new Skywheel at the Boardwalk

© JIM MOREKIS

◖ BAREFOOT LANDING

Before the arrival of Broadway at the Beach was the Strand's original high-concept retail and dining complex, Barefoot Landing (4898 U.S. 17 S., 843/272-8349, www.bflanding.com, hours vary). It's less flashy on the surface and certainly more tasteful, but trust me, it's just as commercial.

The centerpiece of the two-decade-old entertainment and shopping complex is **The Alabama Theatre** (4750 U.S. 17 S., 843/272-5758, www.alabama-theatre.com, ticket prices vary), a project of the famed country-and-western band of the same name, who despite their eponymous roots actually got their start gigging in juke joints in the Grand Strand. A stone's throw away is the **House of Blues** (4640 U.S. 17 S., 843/272-3000, www.hob.com), bringing in name acts on an almost nightly basis as well as diners to its excellent restaurant. On some nights you can pose for a picture with a real live tiger cub on your lap at **T.I.G.E.R.S. Preservation Station** (843/361-4552, www.tigerfriends.com, hours vary). Shopping is mostly the name of the game here, though.

Alligator Adventure

One of the most popular attractions within Barefoot Landing is Alligator Adventure (www.alligatoradventure.com, $18 adults, $12 ages 4-12, free under age 4). They have hundreds of alligators, yes, but also plenty of turtles, tortoises, snakes, and birds. The otters are a big hit as well. The highlight, though, comes during the daily alligator feedings, when you get a chance to see the real power and barely controlled aggression of these magnificent indigenous beasts. Keep in mind that due to the cold-blooded reptiles' dormant winter nature, the feedings are not held in the colder months.

CHILDREN'S MUSEUM OF SOUTH CAROLINA

A less-expensive form of entertainment with an added educational component at Myrtle

© JIM MOREKIS

Alligator Adventure

is the Children's Museum of South Carolina (2501 N. Kings Hwy., 843/946-9469, www.cmsckids.org, summer Mon.-Sat. 9 A.M.-4 P.M., $8). This facility tries hard to compete with the splashier attractions in town but still manages to keep a reasonably strong educational focus with programs like "Crime Lab Chemistry," "World of Art," and "Space Adventures."

FAMILY KINGDOM AMUSEMENT AND WATER PARK

For a taste of old-time beachfront amusement park fun, try the Family Kingdom (300 4th Ave. S., 843/626-3471, www.family-kingdom.com, free admission, cost of rides varies) overlooking the Atlantic Ocean. It boasts several good old-school rides, such as the Sling Shot, the Yo-Yo, and everyone's favorite, the wooden Swamp Fox roller coaster with a crazy 110-foot free fall. The attached Water Park, though not a match to the one at Broadway at the Beach, is

a lot of fun, with the requisite slides and a long "lazy river" floating ride.

As Family Kingdom's marketing is quick to point out, one of the big attractions here is the fact that you can look out over the beach itself. I think one of the best things is that there is no admission charge—you pay by the ride (although all-inclusive wristbands are available starting at $24.50). This means parents and grandparents without the stomach for the rides don't have to pay through the nose just to chauffeur the little ones who do.

RIPLEY'S BELIEVE IT OR NOT!

Distinct in all but name from Ripley's Aquarium at Broadway at the Beach, this combo attraction down in the older area of Myrtle Beach—but very close to the brand-new Boardwalk—features several separate, though more or less adjacent, offerings from the venerable Ripley's franchise.

The **Ripley's Believe It or Not! Odditorium** (901 N. Ocean Blvd., 843/448-2331, www.ripleys.com, Sun.-Thurs. 10 A.M.-10 P.M., Fri.-Sat. 10 A.M.-11 P.M., $15 adults, $8 ages 6-11, free under age 6) is your typical Ripley's repository of strange artifacts from around the world, updated with video and computer graphics for the new generation.

Ripley's Haunted Adventure (915 N. Ocean Blvd., 843/448-2331, www.ripleys.com, Sun.-Thurs. noon-10 P.M., Fri.-Sat. noon-11 P.M., $14 adults, $8 ages 6-11, free under age 6) is a sort of scaled-down version of Disney's famous Haunted House ride, with live actors scaring you through three floors.

Ripley's Moving Theater (917 N. Ocean Blvd., 843/448-2331, www.ripleys.com, Sun.-Thurs. 10 A.M.-10 P.M., Fri.-Sat. 10 A.M.-11 P.M., $14 adults, $8 ages 6-11, free under age 6) is a combined ride and movie theater featuring two motion-oriented films screened on a self-contained human conveyor belt, with a sort of kinetic IMAX effect.

WACCATEE ZOOLOGICAL FARM

The closest thing to a bona fide zoo in Myrtle is Waccatee Zoological Farm (8500 Enterprise Rd., 843/650-8500, www.waccateezoo.com,

Ripley's Believe It or Not!

daily 10 A.M.-5 P.M., $9 adults, $4 ages 1-12). A humble affair by comparison to the state's premier zoo in Columbia, Waccatee is a totally private venture on 500 acres of land about 15 minutes' drive out of town. There are buffalo, zebras, kangaroos, and emus, many of which the kids will enjoy feeding for a few bucks per bag.

Animal activists be forewarned: Many of the animals are kept in enclosed spaces, and there is a noticeable lack of professionally trained staff.

◖ OCEAN DRIVE BEACH

Less an actual place than a state of mind, the "OD" up in North Myrtle Beach is notable for its role in spawning one of America's great musical genres, beach music. Don't confuse beach music with the Beach Boys or Dick Dale— that's surf music. Beach music, simply put, is music to dance the shag to. Think the Drifters, the Platters, and the Swingin' Medallions.

To experience the OD, go to the intersection of Ocean Boulevard and Main Street and take in the vibe. There's still major shag action going on up here, specifically at several clubs specializing in the genre. If you don't want to shag, don't worry—this is still a charming, laid-back area that's a lot of fun simply to stroll around and enjoy a hot dog or ice cream cone.

CHERRY GROVE PIER

One of the few grand old pavilions left on the southeast coast, North Myrtle's Cherry Grove Pier (3500 N. Ocean Blvd., 843/249-1625, www.cherrygrovepier.com, Sun.-Thurs. 6 A.M.-midnight, 6 A.M.-2 A.M. Fri.-Sat.) was built in the 1950s. Despite remodeling in the late 1990s, it still retains that nostalgic feel, with anglers casting into the waters and kids eating ice cream cones. There's a neat two-story observation deck, and on a clear day you can see North Carolina.

Unusually, this is a privately owned pier. It's particularly popular with anglers, who have their state licensing needs covered by the pier.

Get bait or rent a fishing rod ($20 per day plus refundable $50 deposit) at the **Tackle and Gift Shop** (843/249-1625). They'll also sell you a crab net to cast off the pier ($6, with licenses and permits included).

LA BELLE AMIE VINEYARD

The only vineyard on the Strand, the peaceful and scenic La Belle Amie Vineyard (1120 St. Joseph Rd., 843/399-9463, www.labelleamie. com, Mon.-Sat. 10 A.M.-6 P.M.) in Little River is owned by two sisters, Vicki Weigle and June Bayman, who are descended from this old tobacco plantation's owners (in French the vineyard's name means "beautiful friend," but it's also a play on the family name, Bellamy). You can purchase wine for your own enjoyment or for gifts, or you can just visit the tasting room (Mon.-Sat. 10 A.M.-4:30 P.M.), where a mere $5 pp gets you a sampling of any five wines. Coupons for discounted purchase are available at the tasting room.

TOURS

The number of tours offered in Myrtle Beach is nothing compared to Charleston, this being much more of a "doing" place than a "seeing" place. The most fun and comprehensive tour in the area is **Coastal Safari Jeep Tours** (843/497-5330, www.carolinasafari.com, $38 adults, $20 children), which takes you on a guided tour in a super-size jeep (holding 12-14 people). You'll go well off the commercial path to see such sights on the Waccamaw Neck as old plantations, Civil War sites, and slave cabins as well as hear lots of ghost stories. They'll pick you up at most area hotels.

Entertainment and Events

NIGHTLIFE

Any discussion of Myrtle Beach nightlife must begin with a nod to **The Bowery** (110 9th Ave. N., 843/626-3445, www.thebowerybar.com, 11 A.M.-2 A.M. daily), a country-and-western and Southern-rock spot right off the beach, which has survived several hurricanes since opening in 1944. Its roadhouse-style decor hasn't changed a whole lot since then, other than some cheesy marketing to play up its role in history as the place where the country band Alabama got its start playing for tips in 1973 under the name Wildcountry. They were still playing gigs here when their first hit, "Tennessee River," hit the charts in 1980.

Bands usually crank up here around 9 P.M., and there is a nominal cover charge. There's only one type of draft beer served at The Bowery, at $2.50 per mug, and there is no real dance floor to speak of. If the proud display of Confederate flags doesn't bother you, it's usually a lot of fun.

Once overlooking the now-razed historic Myrtle Beach Pavilion, as of this writing The Bowery is fronted by an empty lot that will presumably be filled by a more modern attraction; if history is any guide, The Bowery will probably outlive it as well. Right next door is The Bowery's "sister bar," **Duffy's** (110 9th Ave. N., 843/626-3445), owned by the same folks and with a similarly down-home vibe, except without the live music.

For a more upscale if definitely less personal and unique experience, Broadway at the Beach hosts the high-profile (some say overrated) national clubs **Planet Hollywood** (2915 Hollywood Dr., 843/448-7827, www.planethollywood.com, hours vary by season) and the **Hard Rock Cafe** (1322 Celebrity Circle, 843/946-0007, www.hardrock.com, Mon.-Sun. 11 A.M.-midnight).

You don't have to be a Parrothead to enjoy **Jimmy Buffett's Margaritaville** (1114

The Bowery, where country band Alabama got its start

Celebrity Circle, 843/448-5455, www.margaritaville.com, daily 11 A.M.-midnight) at Broadway at the Beach, actually a pretty enjoyable experience considering it's a national chain. The eponymous margaritas are, of course, the beverage highlight, but they also serve Jimmy's signature LandShark Lager on tap for the beer lovers.

Nearby is the techno- and house music-oriented **Club Kryptonite** (2925 Hollywood Dr., 843/839-9200, www.club-kryptonite.com), more of a full-on nightclub with DJs in both the main room and in the more intimate Cherry Martini Lounge. Hours can be erratic during the off-season.

In addition to its attached live performance space, the **House of Blues** (4640 U.S. 17, 843/272-3000, www.hob.com) at Barefoot Landing features a hopping bar in its dining area, situated amid a plethora of folk art reminiscent of the Mississippi Delta. Most nights feature live entertainment on a small stage starting at about 10 P.M.

SHAG DANCING

North Myrtle Beach is the nexus of that Carolina-based dance known as the shag. There are several clubs in town that have made a name for themselves as the unofficial "shag clubs" of South Carolina. The two main ones are **Duck's** (229 Main St., 843/249-3858, www.ducksatoceandrive.com) and **Fat Harold's** (210 Main St., 843/249-5779, www.fatharolds.com). There's also **The Pirate's Cove** (205 Main St., 843/249-8942).

Another fondly regarded spot is the **OD Pavilion** (91 S. Ocean Blvd., 843/280-0715), a.k.a. the Sunset Grill or "Pam's Palace," on the same site as the old Roberts Pavilion that was destroyed by 1954's Hurricane Hazel. Legend has it this was where the shag was born. Also in North Myrtle, the **Ocean Drive Beach Club** (100 S. Ocean Blvd., 843/249-6460), a.k.a. "the OD Lounge," inside the Ocean Drive Beach and Golf Resort, specializes in shag dancing most days after 4 P.M. The resort is a focal point of local shag conventions and is even home to the **Shaggers Hall of Fame.** Also inside the Ocean Drive Resort is another popular shag club, **The Spanish Galleon** (100 N. Ocean Blvd., 843/249-1047), a.k.a. "The Galleon."

Key local shag events, which are quite well attended, include the **National Shag Dance Championships** (www.shagnationals.com, Jan.-Mar.), the **Spring Safari** (www.shagdance.com, Apr.), and the **Fall Migration** (www.shagdance.com, mid-Sept.).

THE ARTS
Carolina Opry

Nothing can duplicate the experience of the Grand Ole Opry in Nashville, but don't snicker at Myrtle's Carolina Opry (8901-A Business U.S. 17, 800/843-6779, www.thecarolinaopry.com, showtimes and ticket prices vary). Since 1986 this well-respected stage show, begun by legendary promoter Calvin Gilmore, has packed 'em in at the Grand Strand. It is a hoot for country music fans and city slickers alike.

The main focus is the regular Opry show, done in the classic, free-wheeling, fast-moving variety format known to generations of old-school country fans from the original Opry. Some of the humor is corny, and the brief but open displays of patriotic and faith-based music aren't necessarily for everyone and might be slightly confusing given the emphasis on sexy and accomplished female dancers. But there's no arguing the high energy and vocal and instrumental abilities of these very professional singers, instrumentalists, and dancers, who gamely take on hits through the generations ranging from bluegrass to Motown, pop, and modern country.

The Carolina Opry augments its regular music, comedy, and dance show with a seasonal Christmas special, which is highly popular and sells out even faster than the regular shows, often six or more months in advance. There is generally one other bit of specialty programming each year, such as the recent *Good Vibrations* pop hits revue.

The 2,200-seat Carolina Opry theater, while no match for Nashville's classic Ryman Auditorium, is pretty classy for a venue only built in 1992.

Legends in Concert

Way down in Surfside Beach, where the big buildup on the Strand begins, you'll find *Legends in Concert* (301 Business U.S. 17, 843/238-7827, www.legendsinconcert.com, prices vary), a popular rotating show of celebrity impersonators from Elvis to Barbra Streisand. As cheesy as that sounds, the resemblances can be quite uncanny, and the shows are quite entertaining.

House of Blues

Besides being a great place for dinner, on the other side of the restaurant is the stage for the House of Blues (4640 U.S. 17 S., 843/272-3000, www.hob.com, prices vary) at Barefoot Landing in North Myrtle Beach. They bring some pretty happening names in R&B, straight blues, and rock-and-roll to this fun venue dedicated to preserving old-school music and live performance.

Medieval Times

Oh, come on—what's not to like about bountiful feasts, juggling jesters, skillful falconers, fetching maidens, and brave jousting knights? At Medieval Times (2904 Fantasy Way, 843/236-4635, www.medievaltimes.com, $51 adults, $31 under age 13) you'll get all that and more. The kitsch quotient is high at this Renaissance Faire on steroids, a live-action story line featuring plenty of stage combat, music, and a steady stream of culinary items for your enjoyment (and yes, there's a full bar for those of drinking age). But there's an honest-to-goodness educational element as well: You'll be eating everything with your hands—no utensils in the 11th century—and most of the action and history is roughly authentic. The price may seem high at first glance, but keep in mind you're getting a hearty full dinner plus a two-hour stage show.

THE STORY OF THE SHAG

Judy's House of Oldies deals in rare shag music recordings.

In South Carolina, the shag is neither a type of rug nor what Austin Powers does in his spare time. It's a dance—a smooth, laid-back, happy dance done to that equally smooth, laid-back, happy kind of rhythm-and-blues called beach music (not to be confused with surf music such as the Beach Boys). The boys twirl the girls while their feet kick and slide around with a minimum of upper-body movement—the better to stay cool in the Carolina heat.

Descended from the Charleston, another indigenous Palmetto State dance, the shag originated on the Strand sometime in the 1930s, when the popular Collegiate Shag was slowed down to the subgenre now called the Carolina Shag. While shag scholars differ as to the exact spawning ground, there's a consensus that North Myrtle Beach's Ocean Drive, or "OD" in local patois, became the home of the modern shag sometime in the mid-1940s.

Legend has it that the real shag was born when white teenagers, "jumping the Jim Crow rope" by watching dancers at black nightclubs in the segregated South, brought those moves back to the beach and added their own twists.

Indeed, while the shag has always been primarily practiced by white people, many of the leading beach music bands were (and still are) African American.

By the mid-late 1950s the shag, often called simply "the basic" or "the fas' dance," was all the rage with the Strand's young people, who gathered at beachfront pavilions and in local juke joints called beach clubs, courting each other to the sounds of early beach music greats like the Drifters, the Clovers, and Maurice Williams and the Zodiacs. This is the time period most fondly remembered by today's shaggers, a time of penny loafers (no socks!), poodle skirts, and 45-rpm records, when the sea breeze was the only air-conditioning.

The shag is practiced today by a graying but devoted cadre of older fans, with a vanguard of younger practitioners keeping the art form alive. A coterie of North Myrtle clubs specializes in the dance, while the area hosts several large-scale gatherings of shag aficionados each year.

To immerse yourself in shag culture, head on up to Ocean Drive Beach in North Myrtle at the intersection of Ocean Boulevard and Main Street and look down at the platters in the sidewalk marking the **Shaggers Walk of Fame.** Walk a couple of blocks up to the corner of Main Street and Hillside Drive and visit the mecca of beach music stores, **Judy's House of Oldies** (300 Main St., 843/249-8649, www.judyshouseofoldies.com, Mon.-Sat. 9 A.M.-6 P.M.). They also sell instructional DVDs.

To get a taste of the dance itself, stop by the **OD Pavilion** (91 S. Ocean Blvd., 843/280-0715), **Duck's** (229 Main St., 843/249-3858, www.ducksatoceandrive.com), or **Fat Harolds** (210 Main St., 843/249-5779, www.fatharolds.com), or visit **The Spanish Galleon** (100 N. Ocean Blvd., 843/249-1047) inside the Ocean Drive Beach Resort. If you're interested, don't be shy. Shaggers are notoriously gregarious and eager to show off their stock-in-trade. It's easy to learn, it's family-friendly, and there will be no shortage of pleasant young-at-heart shaggers around who will be happy to teach you the steps.

Carolina Opry

Pirate's Voyage

Sharing a parking lot with the Carolina Opry is Pirate's Voyage (8901-B N. Kings Hwy., 843/497-9700, www.piratesvoyage.com, $42 adults, $22 ages 4-11), the newest entertainment attraction to hit Myrtle Beach. Affiliated with Dolly Parton's entertainment empire—her "Dixie Stampede" originally occupied this building—Pirate's Voyage takes you on a rollicking two-hour trip into the world of buccaneers, with fighting, lost treasure, dancing, acrobatics, mermaids, and assorted high-seas drama, all with photographers on hand to document your experience...for a price, me hearties. Like Medieval Times, this is essentially dinner theater with three shows a day in the high season of late summer, offering a variety of suitably swashbuckling menu items like chicken, pork, and fried shrimp. OK, so you don't come here for the food.

The Alabama Theatre

The Alabama Theatre (4750 U.S. 17, 843/272-5758, www.alabama-theatre.com, ticket prices vary) at Barefoot Landing in North Myrtle Beach focuses on the long-running song-and-dance revue *One: The Show* as well as big-name acts who may be past their prime but are still able to fill seats, such as the Oakridge Boys, George Jones, Kenny Rogers, and, of course, the eponymous troubadours Alabama, who got their big break while playing at Myrtle Beach. It's not all country, though—Motown and beach music acts like the Temptations and the Platters are often featured as well. As with the Carolina Opry, Barefoot Landing has its own Christmas special, and as with the Opry's offering, this one sells out well in advance.

Palace Theatre

The Palace Theatre (1420 Celebrity Circle, 800/905-4228, www.palacetheatremyrtlebeach.com, ticket prices vary) at Broadway at the Beach offers a variety of toned-down Vegas-style entertainment. The most recent show was *Le*

Grande Cirque, a family-friendly version of the kind of show made famous by Cirque du Soleil.

CINEMA

At Broadway on the Beach, there's a multiplex, Carmike's **Broadway Cinema 16** (843/445-1600, www.carmike.com). Other movie theaters include the **Cinemark** (2100 Coastal Grand Circle, 843/839-3221, www.cinemark.com) at the Coastal Grand Mall and the massive new **Grand 14 at the Market Common** (4002 Deville St., 843/282-0550) at the multiuse Market Common, actually a repurposed Air Force base.

FESTIVALS AND EVENTS

Interestingly, most events in Myrtle Beach don't happen during the three-month high season of June-August, mostly because it's so darn hot that all anyone wants to do is get in the water.

Winter

The Grand Strand is the birthplace of the dance called the shag, and each winter for the last 25 years the **National Shag Dance Championships** (2000 N. Kings Hwy., 843/497-7369, www.shagnationals.com, from $15 per night) have been the pinnacle of the art form. Beginning with preliminaries in January, contestants in five age ranges compete for a variety of awards, culminating in the finals the first week in March. The level of professionalism might amaze you—for such a lazy-looking dance, these are serious competitors.

Spring

You might not automatically associate our colder neighbor to the north with Myrtle Beach, but **Canadian American Days** (various venues, www.myrtlebeachinfo.com, free), or "Can Am," brings tens of thousands of visitors of both nationalities to sites all over the Strand each March to enjoy a variety of musical and cultural events. Always on top of marketing opportunities, the Myrtle Beach Chamber

House of Blues at Barefoot Landing

of Commerce makes sure this happens during Ontario's spring holidays to ensure maximum north-of-the-border attendance. While most of the events have little or nothing to do with Canada itself, this is basically a great excuse for Canucks to get some Carolina sunshine.

The **Spring Games and Kite Flying Contest** (843/448-7881, free) brings an exciting array of airborne craft to the Strand in front of Broadway on the Beach on an April weekend as the springtime winds peak.

Also in April is the area's second-largest shag event, the **Society of Stranders Spring Safari** (www.shagdance.com). Several clubs in North Myrtle Beach participate in hosting shag dancers from all over for a week of, well, shagging.

The biggest single event in Myrtle Beach happens in May with the **Spring Bike Rally** (various venues, www.myrtlebeachbikeweek.com, free), always known simply as "Bike Week." In this nearly 70-year-old event, over 250,000 Harley-Davidson riders and their

MOTORCYCLE MADNESS

Growling engines? Spinning tires? Patriotic colors? Polished chrome? Bikini car washes? Erotic bull-riding contests? That is the spectacle known as Myrtle Beach Bike Week, one of the largest gatherings of Harley-Davidson enthusiasts on the East Coast and one of the oldest, at about 65 years.

The event has historically happened each May on the weekend before Memorial Day weekend, bringing over 250,000 motorcyclists and their entourages to town for 10 days of riding, bragging, and carousing. South Carolina's lack of a helmet law is a particular draw to these freedom-cherishing motorcyclists. A few days later, on Memorial Day weekend, there's another bike rally, this one simply called Black Bike Week. Nearly as large as the regular Bike Week, the focus is on African American riders and their machines.

Contrary to stereotype, there's not much of an increase in crime during either Bike Week. Regardless, they are widely known as a particularly bad time to bring families to the area, and therein lies the controversy. Joining other municipalities around the nation in discouraging motorcycle rallies, the city of Myrtle Beach has enacted tough measures to force the bike rallies to leave town and make the area more family-friendly during that time. Most controversial among recent measures was a municipal helmet law, enforceable only within Myrtle Beach city limits, that was later struck down by the South Carolina Supreme Court. Other, still-standing measures include stringent noise ordinances designed to include the roaring, rattling tailpipes of pretty much every Harley ever made. The separate municipality of North Myrtle Beach, however, has made it clear that bikers are welcome there even if they're non grata a few miles to the south.

As of now, it seems that the rallies will remain on the Strand rather than gun their collective throttle and head elsewhere, as they occasionally threaten to do when relations with local municipalities and police departments get too tense. The upshot for the nonmotorcyclist visitor? Bikers are somewhat less of a factor than in years past, and certainly local police are taking them more seriously. But the time around Memorial Day is still as crowded as ever.

---

entourages gather to cruise around the place, admire each other's custom rides, and generally party their patooties off. While the typical Harley dude these days is getting on in years and is probably a mild-mannered store manager in regular life, young or old they all do their best to let their hair down at this festive event. Dozens of related events go on throughout the week at venues all over the Strand, from tough-man contests to "foxy boxing" matches to wet T-shirt contests. You get the picture—it's not for the politically correct or for young children.

Summer

Right after the Spring Bike Rally is the **Atlantic Beach Bikefest** (various venues), on Memorial Day weekend, much more commonly referred to as "Black Bike Week." This event started in the 1980s and is spiritually based in Atlantic Beach, formerly the area's "black beach" during the days of segregation. It sees over 200,000 African American motorcycle enthusiasts gather in Myrtle Beach for a similar menu of partying, bikini contests, cruising, and the like. While the existence of separate events often reminds some people of the state's unfortunate history of segregation, supporters of both Bike Week and Black Bike Week insist it's not a big deal, and that bikers of either race are welcome at either event.

Kicking off with a festive parade, the 50-year-old **Sun Fun Festival** (various venues, www.grandstrandevents.com), generally held the weekend after Memorial Day weekend, signals the real beginning of the summer season with bikini contests, Jet Ski races, parades, air shows, and concerts galore.

The **City of Myrtle Beach Independence Day Celebration** (www.cityofmyrtlebeach.com, free) each July 4 weekend is when the largest number of visitors is in Myrtle Beach. It's fun, it's hot, there's fireworks aplenty, and boy, is it crowded.

Fall

For a week in mid-September, North Myrtle Beach hosts one of the world's largest shag dancing celebrations, the **Society of Stranders Fall Migration** (www.shagdance.com, free). Head up to the intersection of Ocean Drive and Main Street to hear the sounds of this unique genre, and party with the shaggers at various local clubs. If you don't know the steps, don't worry—instructors are usually on hand.

There's another, smaller Harley riders' rally the first week in October, the **Fall Motorcycle Rally** (various venues, www.myrtlebeachbikeweek.com, free).

Thanksgiving Day weekend, when the beaches are much less crowded and the hotels much cheaper, is the **South Carolina Bluegrass Festival** (2101 N. Oak St., 706/864-7203, www.aandabluegrass.com, $30 adults, $20 ages 6-13, free under age 6), a delightful and well-attended event at the Myrtle Beach Convention Center, celebrating the Appalachian music tradition in a coastal setting with some of the biggest names in the genre.

Shopping

Shopping on the Grand Strand is strongly destination-oriented. You tend to find shops of similar price points and merchandise types clustered together in convenient locations: Upscale shops are in one place and discount and outlet stores in another. Here's a rundown of the main retail areas on the Strand with some of the standout shops.

BROADWAY AT THE BEACH

The sprawling Broadway at the Beach complex (U.S. 17 Bypass and 21st Ave. N., www.broadwayatthebeach.com, hours vary) has scads of stores, some of which are quite interesting and rise well beyond tourist schlock. There are maps and directories of the site available at various kiosks around the area.

One of my favorite shops is **Retroactive** (843/916-1218, www.shopretroactive.com), a shop specializing in '70s and '80s styles and kitsch, with some of the best (and wittiest) pop-culture T-shirts I've seen. The owners are frank about their continuing obsession with '80s hair bands. Another awesome T-shirt and trinket shop that the kids and teens will particularly enjoy is **Stupid Factory** (843/448-1100). There are lots of mediocre sports apparel stores out there, but **Sports Fanatics** (843/445-2585) has an amazing collection of jerseys, shirts, and lids, primarily focused on pro teams. The kids—and those with a sweet tooth—will go crazy in the aptly named **It'SUGAR** (843/916-1300, www.itsugar.com), a store dedicated to just about any kind of candy and candy-themed merchandise you can think of, from modern brands to retro favorites. If the packaged or bulk varieties don't float your boat, you can design your own massive chocolate bar. And, of course, this being Myrtle Beach, there's a **Harley Davidson** (843/293-5555) gift store with Hog-oriented merch galore.

The bottom line on Broadway at the Beach, though, is that it's made for walking around and browsing. Just bring your walking shoes—the place is huge—and keep in mind that there's not a lot of shade.

a typical storefront at Broadway at the Beach

© JIM MOREKIS

BAREFOOT LANDING

There are over 100 shops at Barefoot Landing (4898 U.S. 17 S., 843/272-8349, www.bflanding.com, hours vary) in North Myrtle Beach—as well as one cool old-fashioned carousel—but perhaps the most unique spot is **T.I.G.E.R.S. Preservation Station** (843/361-4552, www.tigerfriends.com, hours vary), where you get the opportunity to have your picture taken with a live tiger or lion cub. This is the fund-raising arm of a local organization for conservation of the big cats as well as gorillas and monkeys, so the service isn't cheap. Portraits begin at about $60 to pose with a single critter and go up from there depending on the number of animals you want to pose with. However, you don't pay per person, so the whole family can get in the shot for the same price as a child. It may sound like a lot of money, but this is truly a once-in-a-lifetime experience. An attendant takes the animal of your choice out of a spacious holding area, places it on your lap, and a photographer takes

the shot. Sometimes you can hold a milk bottle to the cub's mouth. If you don't want to spring for a photo, you can just watch the frolicking (or more often, slumbering) cubs up close from behind a transparent wall. They're unbelievably cute, as you can imagine.

Just relocated to the Strand from their grape yards in Chester, South Carolina, is **Carolina Vineyards Winery** (843/361-9181, www.carolinavineyards.com). Buy wine as a gift, or taste any seven of their labels for only $3.

There are magic shops, and then there are *magic shops*. **Conley's House of Magic** (843/272-4227, http://conleyshouseofmagic.com) is definitely the latter. Packed in this relatively small space is just about every legendary trick and trick deck known to the magician's art, along with a cool variety of magic books teaching you, in deadly serious fashion, the innermost secrets of the trade. **Toys & Co.** (843/663-0748, www.toysandco.com) carries a wide range of toys and games, with an emphasis

Meet a tiger cub at Barefoot Landing.

on way-cool European-style brands you won't see at the local Wal-Mart.

THE MARKET COMMON

One of the most hotly anticipated and cutting-edge things to hit Myrtle Beach in years, The Market Common (4017 Deville St., www.marketcommonmb.com, hours vary) is an ambitious residential-retail mixed-use development opened for business on the site of the decommissioned Myrtle Beach Air Force Base. While its location near the Myrtle Beach International Airport means it's not exactly amid the sun-and-fun action (possibly a good thing, depending on the season), the very pedestrian-friendly development style and tasteful shops might provide a refreshing change of pace.

There are three dozen (and counting) stores, including Anthropologie, Williams-Sonoma, Copper Penny, Chico's, Brooks Brothers, Fossil, Banana Republic, Barnes & Noble, and Jake and Company ("Life Is Good"). There

are plenty of restaurants, including Ultimate California Pizza and P. F. Chang's, and a large multiplex movie theater.

For those interested in how the sprawling old base was closed in the 1990s and repurposed so completely, there's interpretive signage all around the pedestrian mall and along the roadways leading to it. At the Market Common's entrance is Warbird Park, a well-done veterans memorial featuring an Air Force A-10 attack aircraft, an F-100 Super Sabre, and a Corsair II.

MALLS

The premier mall in the area is **Coastal Grand Mall** (2000 Coastal Grand Circle, 843/839-9100, www.coastalgrand.com, Mon.-Sat. 10 A.M.-9 P.M., Sun. noon-6 P.M.) at the U.S. 17 Bypass and U.S. 501. It's anchored by Belk, J. C. Penney, Sears, Dillard's, and Dick's Sporting Goods.

Your basic meat-and-potatoes mall, **Myrtle Beach Mall** (10177 N. Kings Hwy., 843/272-4040, http://shopmyrtlebeachmall.com,

The Market Common's innovative repurposing of the old Myrtle Beach Air Force Base

Mon.-Sat. 10 A.M.-9 P.M., Sun. noon-6 P.M.) is anchored by Belk, J. C. Penney, and Bass Pro Shops.

DISCOUNT BEACHWEAR

Literally dozens of cavernous, tacky, deep-discount T-shirt-and-towel type places are spread up and down Kings Highway like mushrooms after a rain. The vast majority of them belong to one of several well-established chains: **Eagles Beachwear** (www.eaglesbeachwear.net), **Whales** (www.

whalesnauticalgifts.com), **Wing's Beachwear** (www.wingsbeachwear.com), and **Bargain Beachwear (www.bargainbeachwear.com)** These are the kinds of places to get assorted bric-a-brac and items for your beach visit. The quality isn't that bad, and the prices are uniformly low.

OUTLET MALLS

There are two massive **Tanger Outlets** (www.tangeroutlet.com) at Myrtle Beach: **Tanger Outlet North** (10835 Kings Rd., 843/449-0491) off Kings Road/U.S. 17, and **Tanger Outlet South** (4635 Factory Stores Blvd., 843/236-5100) off U.S. 501. Both offer over 100 factory outlet stores of almost every imaginable segment, from Fossil to Disney, OshKosh B'Gosh to Timberland. Full food courts are available, and many folks easily spend an entire day here.

For years, busloads of hard-core shoppers from throughout the South have taken organized trips to the Grand Strand specifically to shop at **Waccamaw Factory Shoppes** (3071 Waccamaw Blvd., 843/236-8200). Their passion hasn't abated, as new generations of shopaholics get the fever to come here and browse the often deeply discounted offerings at row after row of outlet stores. There are actually two locations, the Factory Shoppes themselves and the nearby **Waccamaw Pottery** (3200 Pottery Dr., 843/236-6152). Bring your walking shoes (or buy some new ones at one of the many shoe stores), but don't worry about getting from one mall to the other—there's a free shuttle.

Sports and Recreation

Myrtle Beach's middle name might as well be recreation. While some of the local variety tends toward overkill—I personally loathe Jet Skis, for example—there's no denying that if it involves outdoor activity, it's probably offered here. For general info, visit www.grandstrandevents.com. For municipal recreation info, visit www.cityofmyrtlebeach.com.

ON THE WATER

Beaches

The center of activity is on the Strand itself: miles of user-friendly beaches. They're not the most beautiful in the world, but they're nice enough, and access is certainly no problem. In Myrtle Beach and North Myrtle Beach, you'll find clearly designated public access points off Ocean Boulevard, some with parking and some without. Both municipalities run well-marked public parking lots at various points, some of which are free during the off-season.

Dog owners will be pleased to know that May 15-September 15, dogs are allowed on the beach before 9 A.M. and after 5 P.M. September 15-May 15, dogs are allowed on the beach at any time of day.

Restrict your swimming to within 150 feet of shore. Surfside Beach to the south is a no-smoking beach with access points at 16th Avenue North, 6th Avenue North, 3rd Avenue North, Surfside Pier, 3rd Avenue South, 4th Avenue South, 13th Avenue South, and Melody Lane.

Surfing

There's a steady, if low-key, surf scene in Myrtle Beach despite the fact that the surfing is not really that good and the sport is restricted to certain areas of the beach during the busy summer season. The rules are a little complicated. In Myrtle Beach proper, surfing is only allowed April 15-September 15 daily 10 A.M.-5 P.M. in the following zones:

- 29th Avenue South to the southern city limits
- 37th Avenue North to 47th Avenue North
- 62nd Avenue North to 68th Avenue North
- 82nd Avenue North to northern city limits

Up in North Myrtle Beach, surfers must stay in the following zones May 15-September 15 daily 9 A.M.-4 P.M.:

- Cherry Grove Pier
- 6th Avenue North
- 13th Avenue South
- 28th Avenue South
- 38th Avenue South

Down at Surfside Beach, surfing is restricted to the following zones, year-round daily 10 A.M.-5 P.M.:

- 12th Avenue North to 14th Avenue North
- Melody Lane to 13th Avenue South

The oldest surf shop in the area, south of Myrtle in Garden City Beach, is the **Village Surf Shoppe** (500 Atlantic Ave., 843/651-6396, www.villagesurf.com), which has catered to the Strand's growing surf scene since 1969. Nearly as old is the **Surf City Surf Shop** (1758 U.S. 17 S., 843/272-1090; 3001 N. Kings Hwy., 843/626-5412, www.surfcitysurfshop.com) franchise in Myrtle proper.

Diving

Diving is popular on the Strand. As with fishing, many trips depart from Little River just above North Myrtle Beach. Offshore features include many historic wrecks, including the post-Civil War wreck of the USS *Sherman* offshore of Little River, and artificial reefs such as the famed "Barracuda Alley," teeming with marine life, off Myrtle Beach.

Coastal Scuba (1901 U.S. 17 S., 843/361-3323, www.coastalscuba.com) in North Myrtle is a large operator, offering several different dive tours.

Parasailing, Windsurfing, and Jet Skis

Ocean Watersports (405 S. Ocean Blvd., 843/445-7777, www.parasailmyrtlebeach.com) takes groups up to six on well-supervised, well-equipped parasailing adventures (about $50 pp), with tandem and triple flights available. Observers can go out on the boat for about $20. They also rent Jet Skis and offer "banana boat" rides ($15) in which a long—yes, banana-shaped—raft, straddled by several riders, is towed by a boat up and down the beach.

Downwind Watersports (2915 S. Ocean Blvd., 843/448-7245, www.downwindsailsmyrtlebeach.com) has similar offerings, with the addition of good old-fashioned sailboat lessons and rentals ($16). Parasailing is about $65 pp single ride, banana boats are $16 for 20 minutes, and Jet Ski rentals about $100 per hour.

Farther up the Strand in North Myrtle, between Cherry Grove Beach and Little River, you'll find **Thomas Outdoors Watersports** (2200 Little River Neck Rd., 843/280-2448, www.mbjetski.com), which rents kayaks in addition to Jet Skis and pontoon boats. They offer several Jet Ski tours ($75-125), including a dolphin-watching trip, as well as all-day kayak rental ($45 pp).

Fishing

Most fishing on the Strand is saltwater, with charters, most based in Little River, taking anglers well into Atlantic waters. Tuna, wahoo, mackerel, and dolphin (not the mammal!) are big in the hot months, while snapper and grouper are caught year-round but are best in the colder months.

A good operator up in Little River is **Longway Fishing Charters** (843/249-7813, www.longwaycharters.com), which specializes in offshore fishing. Another in the same area is **Capt. Smiley's Inshore Fishing** (843/361-7445, www.captainsmileyfishingcharters.com). **Fish Hook Charters** (2200 Little River Neck Rd., 843/283-7692, www.fishhookcharters.com) takes a 34-foot boat out from North Myrtle Beach.

For surf fishing on the beach, you do not need a license of any type. All other types of fishing require a valid South Carolina fishing license, available for a nominal fee online (http://dnr.sc.gov) or at any tackle shop and most grocery stores.

Cruises

Except in the winter months, there are plenty of places to cruise in the Strand, from Little River down to Murrells Inlet, from the Waccamaw River to the Intracoastal Waterway. The **Great American Riverboat Company** (8496 Enterprise Rd., 843/650-6600, www.mbriverboat.com) offers sightseeing and dinner cruises along the Intracoastal Waterway. **Island Song Charters** (4374 Landing Rd., 843/467-7088, www.islandsongcharters.com) out of Little River takes you on sunset and dolphin cruises on the 32-foot sailboat *Island Song.*

Up in North Myrtle, **Getaway Adventures** (843/663-1100, www.myrtlebeachboatcruises.com) specializes in dolphin tours. Also in North Myrtle, **Thomas Outdoors Watersports** (2200 Little River Neck Rd., 843/280-2448, www.mbjetski.com) runs dolphin cruises.

ON LAND
Golf

The Grand Strand in general, and Myrtle Beach in particular, is world golf central. There are over 120 courses in this comparatively small area, and if golfers can't find something they like here, they need to sell their clubs. While the number of truly great courses is few—the best courses are farther down the Strand near Pawleys Island—the quality overall is still quite high.

A great bonus is affordability. Partially because of dramatically increased competition due to the glut of courses, and partially because of savvy regional marketing, green fees here are significantly lower than you might expect, in many cases under $100. For even more savings, finding a golf-lodging package deal in Myrtle

Beach is like finding sand on the beach—almost too easy. Check with your hotel to see if they offer any golf packages. At any time of year, some good one-stop shops on the Internet are at www.mbn.com and www.myrtlebeachgolf.com.

Some highlights of area golf include the Davis Love III-designed course at **Barefoot Resort** (4980 Barefoot Resort Ridge Rd., 843/390-3200, www.barefootgolf.com, $105-185) in North Myrtle, maybe the best in the Strand outside Pawleys Island. Or would that be the Greg Norman course, or the Tom Fazio course, or the Pete Dye course, all also at Barefoot? You get the picture.

Also up near North Myrtle is a favorite with visitors and locals alike, the challenging **Glen Dornoch Golf Club** (4840 Glen Dornoch Way, 800/717-8784, www.glensgolfgroup.com, from $100), on 260 beautiful acres. Affiliated with Glen Dornoch are the 27 holes at Little River's **Heather Glen** (4650 Heather Glen Way, 800/868-4536, www.glensgolfgroup.com), which are divided into Red, White, and Blue courses. They combine for what's consistently rated one of the best public courses in the United States.

And no list of area golf is complete without a nod to **Myrtle Beach National** (4900 National Dr., 843/347-4298, www.mbn.com, from $80). With three distinct courses—King's North, West, and South Creek, with its South Carolina-shaped sand trap at hole 3—the National is one of the state's legendary courses, not to mention a heck of a deal.

Miniature Golf

Don't scoff—miniature golf, or "putt-putt" to an older generation, is a big deal in Myrtle Beach. If you thought there were a lot of regular golf courses here, the 50 miniature golf courses will also blow your mind. Sadly, almost all of the classic old-school miniature golf courses are no more, victims of the demand for increased production values and modernized gimmick

holes. But here are some of the standouts, including the best of the North Myrtle courses as well; prices listed are for 18 holes.

The most garishly wonderful course is the completely over-the-top **Mount Atlanticus Minotaur Goff** (707 N. Kings Hwy., 843/444-1008, www.mountatlanticus.com, $10) down near the older section of Myrtle. And yes, that's how it's spelled—get it? Legend has it that this one course cost $3 million to build. Literally the stuff of dreams—or maybe hallucinations—this sprawling course mixes the mythological with the nautical to wonderful effect. You don't actually encounter the Minotaur until the bonus 19th hole, a fiendish water trap. If you get a hole in one, you get free golf here for life.

Hawaiian Rumble (3210 U.S. 17, 843/458-2585, www.prominigolf.com) in North Myrtle is not only a heck of a fun, attractive course, it's also the headquarters of the official training center for the U.S. Professional Miniature Golf Association (the folks who generally get a hole in one on every hole). The Rumble's sister course is **Hawaiian Village** (4205 U.S. 17, 843/361-9629, www.prominigolf.com) in North Myrtle, which is also the home of serious professional miniature golf competitions.

For a bit of retro action, try **Rainbow Falls** (9550 Kings Hwy., 843/497-2557). It's not as garish as some of the newer courses, but fans of old-school putt-putt will love it.

While at Broadway at the Beach, you might want to try the popular medieval-themed **Dragon's Lair** (1197 Celebrity Circle, 843/913-9301, hours vary by season). Yep, it has a 30-foot fire-breathing dragon, Sir Alfred, that you have to make your way around. While the dinosaur craze has cooled somewhat, the golf at **Jurassic Golf** (445 29th Ave., 843/448-2116), festooned with dozens of velociraptors and the like, certainly has stayed hot. There is a similarly themed site in North Myrtle, the new **Dinosaur Adventure** (700 7th Ave., 843/272-8041).

Tennis

There are over 200 tennis courts in the Myrtle Beach area. The main municipal site is the **Myrtle Beach Tennis Center** (3302 Robert Grissom Pkwy., 843/918-2440, www.myrtlebeachtennis.com, $2 pp per hour), which has 10 courts, eight of them lighted. The city also runs six lighted courts at **Midway Park** (U.S. 17 and 19th Ave. S.).

The privately owned **Kingston Plantation** (843/497-2444, www.kingstonplantation.com) specializes in tennis vacations, and you don't even have to be a guest. They have a pro on staff and offer lessons. Down in Pawleys Island, the **Litchfield Beach and Golf Resort** (14276 Ocean Hwy., 866/538-0187, www.litchfieldbeach.com) has two dozen nice courts.

Cycling

In Myrtle Beach, when they say "biker," they mean a Harley dude. Bicycling—or safe bicycling, anyway—is largely limited to fat-tire riding along the beach and easy pedaling through the quiet residential neighborhoods near Little River. There is a bike lane on North Ocean Boulevard from about 29th Avenue North to about 82nd Avenue North. Riding on the sidewalk is strictly prohibited.

As for bike rentals, a good operator is **Beach Bike Shop** (711 Broadway St., 843/448-5335, www.beachbikeshop.com). In North Myrtle, try **Wheel Fun Rentals** (91 S. Ocean Blvd., 843/280-7900, www.wheelfunrentals.com).

Horseback Riding

A horse ride along the surf is a nearly iconic image of South Carolina, combining two of the state's chief pursuits: equestrian sports and hanging out on the beach. A great way to enjoy a horseback ride along the Grand Strand without having to bring your own equine is to check out **Horseback Riding of Myrtle Beach** (843/294-1712, www.myrtlebeachhorserides.com). They offer a variety of group rides, each with a guide, going to nature-preserve or beach locales. While they'll take you out any day of the week, advance reservations are required. Ninety minutes on a nature preserve costs about $50 pp, while a 90-minute ride on the beach is about $75 pp.

You can go horseback riding on Myrtle Beach from the third Saturday in November until the end of February, with these conditions: You must access the beach from Myrtle Beach State Park, you cannot ride over sand dunes in any way, and you must clean up after your horse.

SPECTATOR SPORTS

Playing April-early September in a large new stadium near Broadway at the Beach are the **Myrtle Beach Pelicans** (1251 21st Ave. N., 843/918-6000, www.myrtlebeachpelicans.com, $8-11), a single-A affiliate of the Atlanta Braves playing in the Carolina League.

NASCAR fans already know of the **Myrtle Beach Speedway** (455 Hospitality Lane, www.myrtlebeachspeedway.com, $12, free under age 10) off U.S. 501, one of the more vintage tracks in the country, dating back to 1958 (it was actually a dirt track well into the 1970s). Currently the main draw are the NASCAR Whelen All-American Series races (Apr.-Nov. Sat. 7:30 P.M.).

Other spectator sports in the area tend to revolve around the Chanticleer teams of **Coastal Carolina University** (132 Chanticleer Dr. W., 843/347-8499, www.goccusports.com) just inland from Myrtle Beach in Conway. They play football in the Big South Conference. By the way, *chanticleer* is an old name for a rooster, and in this case is a self-conscious derivative of the mascot of the University of South Carolina, the gamecock.

Accommodations

There is no dearth of lodging in the Myrtle Beach area, from the typical high-rise "resorts" (think condos on steroids) to chain hotels, vacation villas, house rentals, and camping. Because of the plethora of options, prices are generally reasonable, and competition to provide more and more on-site amenities—free breakfasts, "lazy river" pools, washers and dryers, hot tubs, poolside grills, and so on—has only increased. You are the beneficiary, so you might as well take advantage of it.

Note that the stated price range may be very broad because so many Myrtle Beach lodgings offer several room options, from one-bed guest rooms to full three-bedroom suites. Here are a few general tips to consider when booking a room:

- The larger suites are generally "condo apartments," meaning they're privately owned. While they're usually immaculately clean for your arrival, it means that housekeeping is minimal and you won't get lots of complimentary goodies whenever you call the front desk.

- The entire Myrtle Beach area is undergoing growth, and that includes the accommodations. This means that many properties have older sections and newer ones. Ask beforehand which section you're being booked in.

- Check www.myrtlebeachhotels.com for last-minute deals and specials at 11 well-run local resorts.

- By the end of September, prices drop dramatically.

- Almost all area lodgings, especially the high-rises, feature on-site pools galore, lounge chairs and tables are at a premium and go very quickly during high season when the sun's out.

- Always keep in mind that summer is the high season here, unlike the rest of South Carolina, and guest rooms, especially at beachfront places, get snapped up very early.

UNDER $150

For 75 years, **⬛ Driftwood on the Oceanfront** (1600 N. Ocean Blvd., 843/448-1544, www.

driftwoodlodge.com, $100-120) has been a favorite place to stay. Upgraded over the years, but not *too* upgraded, this low five-story 90-room complex is family-owned and takes pride in delivering personalized service that is simply impossible to attain in the larger high-rises nearby. As you'd expect, the guest rooms and suites are a bit on the small side by modern Myrtle Beach standards—with none of the increasingly popular three-bedroom suites available—but most everyone is impressed by the value.

Probably the best-regarded bed-and-breakfast in Myrtle Beach (yes, there are a precious few) is the **⬛ Serendipity Inn** (407 71st Ave. N., 843/449-5268, www.serendipityinn.com, $90-150). A short walk from the beach but sometimes seemingly light years away from the typical Myrtle sprawl, this 15-room gem features a simple but elegant pool, an attractive courtyard, and sumptuous guest rooms. The full breakfast is simple but hearty. There's free Wi-Fi throughout the property.

If you're looking for a basic, inexpensive, one-bed hotel experience on the beach, ask for a room at the new oceanfront section of the **Best Western Grand Strand Inn and Suites** (1804 S. Ocean Blvd., 843/448-1461, $80-140), a smallish but clean and attentively run chain hotel. The property's other buildings are significantly older and are located across busy Ocean Boulevard, and the walk across the street to the beach can be difficult, especially if you have small kids. That said, this is a great value and a quality property.

If water park-style entertainment is your thing, try **Dunes Village Resort** (5200 N. Ocean Blvd., 877/828-2237, www.dunesvillage.com, $140-300), also one of the better values in Myrtle. Its huge indoor water park has copious waterslides, including several for adults, and various other aquatic diversions.

Poolside relaxation is everywhere in Myrtle Beach.

The buildings themselves—the property comprises two high-rise towers—are new and well-equipped, although since this is a timeshare-style property, housekeeping is minimal.

$150-300

My favorite place to stay at Myrtle Beach is the **◖Island Vista Oceanfront Resort** (6000 N. Ocean Blvd., 888/733-7581, www.islandvista. com). While not the flashiest or heaviest in amenities by any means, Island Vista's location in a quiet residential area overlooking a mile of the Strand's best and least-traveled beach makes it a standout alternative to the often crowded and logistically challenging environment you'll find in the more built-up high-rise blocks farther south on the beach. In the high season you'll be paying about $300 for a one-bedroom suite, but the prices on the spacious and very well-equipped two- and three-bedroom suites are competitive. They have the usual multiple-pool option, including an indoor heated pool

area. A big plus is the fact that the in-house fine-dining restaurant, the **Cypress Room,** is a definite cut above most area hotel kitchens.

Consistently one of the best-regarded properties in Myrtle proper, the **Hampton Inn & Suites Oceanfront** (1803 S. Ocean Blvd., 843/946-6400, www.hamptoninnoceanfront. com, $169-259) has been made even better by a recent and thorough upgrade. This is a classic beachfront high-rise (not to be confused with the Hampton Inn at Broadway at the Beach), clean inside and out, with elegant tasteful guest rooms in various sizes (yes, flat-screen TVs were part of the makeover). Guest rooms range from typical one-bed, one-bath hotel-style rooms to larger condo-style suites with a fridge.

Situated more toward North Myrtle and hence closer to those attractions, the **Sea Watch Resort** (161 Sea Watch Blvd., $171-395) is a good choice for those who want the full-on condo high-rise Myrtle Beach experience but not necessarily the crowds that usually go with it. The guest rooms are clean and well-equipped, and by edging north a little on the beach, you can actually spread out and enjoy some breathing room.

An oldie but a goodie, the beachfront **Carolina Winds** (200 76th Ave. N., 843/497-5648, www.carolinawinds.com, $150-300) remains one of the better overall condo-style vacation spots in Myrtle. Unlike many of the newer monolithic high-rises, Carolina Winds almost has a retro Miami Beach feel to it, both in architecture and attitude. A two-night minimum stay is required during the high season.

One of the better-quality stays for the price in Myrtle is the **Roxanne Towers** (1604 N. Ocean Blvd., 843/839-1016, www.theroxanne.com, $150-250). Known for attentive service, this is a busy property in a busy area. Parking is historically something of a problem. Keep in mind that room size is capped at two bedrooms, so there are none of the sprawling three-bedroom suites that many other local places have.

For a quality stay in the heart of Myrtle's beach bustle, go for the **Sandy Beach Resort** (201 S. Ocean Blvd., 800/844-6534, www.beachtrips.com, $200-300). The guest rooms are top-notch, and the service professional. As is the case with many local properties, there is a newer section, the Palmetto Tower, and an "old" section, the venerable Magnolia Tower. There are one-, two-, and three-bedroom units available, the latter a particularly good value.

Considered one of the major remaining centers of the shag subculture on the Strand, the **Ocean Drive Beach and Golf Resort** (98 N. Ocean Blvd., $200-350) up in North Myrtle Beach hosts many events surrounding the notable regional dance, including the Shaggers Hall of Fame. Its on-site lounge, **The Spanish Galleon,** specializes in beach music. It's also just a great place to stay, with amenities such as a "lazy river," a whirlpool, full galley-style kitchens, and, of course, extreme proximity to the beach. A remodel in 2007 has made it even plusher inside and out.

Also up in North Myrtle is the new ◀ **Tilghman Beach and Golf Resort** (1819 Ocean Blvd., 843/280-0913, www.tilghmanresort.com, $200-350), owned by the same company as the Ocean Drive Beach Resort. It's not directly on the beach, but since the buildings in front of it are pretty low, you can still get awesome ocean views. Even the views from the back of the building aren't bad, since they overlook a golf course. But you don't have to be a duffer to enjoy the Tilghman—the pool scene is great, the balconies are roomy, and the suites are huge and well enough equipped (a flat-screen TV in every room) to make you feel right at home.

VACATION RENTALS

There are hundreds, probably thousands, of privately rented condo-style lodgings at Myrtle Beach, in all shapes and forms. Most, however, do a great job of catering to what vacationers here really seem to want: space, convenience, and a working kitchen. All rental agencies basically work with the same listings, so looking for and finding a rental is easier than you might think.

Some of the key brokers are **Myrtle Beach Vacation Rentals** (800/845-0833, www.mb-vacationrentals.com), **Beach Vacations** (866/453-4818, www.beachvacationsmb.com), **Barefoot Vacations** (800/845-0837, www.barefootvacations.info), **Elliott Realty and Beach Rentals** (www.elliottrealty.com), and **Atlantic Dunes Vacation Rentals** (866/544-2568, www.atlanticdunesvacations.com).

CAMPING

Let's start off with what should be obvious by now: Myrtle Beach is not where you go for a pristine quiet camping experience. For that, I suggest Huntington State Park down near Murrells Inlet. However, there is plenty of camping, almost all of it heavily RV-oriented, if you want it. For more info, visit www.campmyrtlebeach.com.

The closest thing to a real live campground

is good old **Myrtle Beach State Park** (4401 S. Kings Hwy., 843/238-5325, www.southcaro-linaparks.com, daily 6 A.M.-10 P.M., $4 adults, $1.50 ages 6-15, free under age 6), which despite being only a short drive from the rest of the beachfront sprawl is still a fairly relaxing place to stay, complete with its own scenic fishing pier (daily fishing fee $4.50). There's even a nature center with a little aquarium and exhibits.

The charming and educational atmosphere is largely due to the fact that this is one of the 17 Civilian Conservation Corps parks, built during the Great Depression and still lovingly maintained by the state of South Carolina. There are four cabins ($54-125) available, all fully furnished and about 200 yards from the beach. The main campground is about 300 yards from the beach and comprises 300 sites

with electricity and water ($23-25) and a 45-site tent and overflow campground ($17-19), which is only open during the summer high season.

The **Myrtle Beach KOA** (613 6th Ave. S., 800/562-7790, www.myrtlebeach-koa.com), though not at all cheap ($40-50 even for tenters), offers the usual safe, dependable amenities of that well-known chain, including rental "kabins" and activities for kids.

Willow Tree RV Resort and Campground (520 Southern Sights Dr., 843/756-4334, www.willowtreervr.com) is set inland on a well-wooded 300-acre tract with large sites well away from the sprawl and offers lakeside fishing and bike trails. In the summer high season, basic sites are $50-82, and the one- and two-bedroom cabins range $120-190.

Food

There are about 2,000 restaurants in the Myrtle Beach area, not counting hotel room service and buffets. You can find any dining option that floats your boat at almost any price level. Seafood, of course, is big and is heartily recommended. But there are steak houses, rib joints, pizza places, and vegetarian restaurants galore as well. We can only explore a small fraction here, but following is a breakdown of some of the more unique and tasty experiences on this bustling part of the Grand Strand.

BREAKFAST
Pancakes are big on the Strand, with many flapjack places open daily 24 hours to accommodate partiers and night owls. If you've got a hankering, just drive up and down Kings Highway/ U.S. 17 long enough and you're bound to find a place. A prime purveyor of pancakes is **Harry's Breakfast Pancakes** (2306 N. Kings Hwy., 843/448-8013, www.harryspancake.com, daily 5:30 A.M.-2 P.M., $4-10). They're not open all

day, but there's enough time to enjoy their fluffy stacks and rich omelets.

BARBECUE, BURGERS, AND STEAKS
The best barbecue in town—and a delightfully low-key experience in this often too-flashy area—is at ◖ **Little Pigs Barbecue** (6102 Frontage Rd., 843/692-9774, Mon.-Sat. 11 A.M.-8 P.M., $8-12). This is a local-heavy place dealing in no-frills pulled pork, piled high at the counter and reasonably priced with a selection of sauces. The lack of atmosphere *is* the atmosphere, and they prefer to let the barbecue (and the hushpuppies and onion rings) do the talking.

Since opening 20 years ago, ◖ **Thoroughbreds** (9706 N. Kings Hwy., 843/497-2636, www.thoroughbredsrestaurant.com, Sun.-Thurs. 5-10 P.M., Fri.-Sat. 5-11 P.M., $20), on the old Restaurant Row, has been considered the premier fine-dining place in Myrtle Beach, dealing in the kind of wood-heavy, clubby, Old World-meets-New World ambience you'd expect to see in Palm Beach, Florida. That said, the prices are definitely more Myrtle Beach; you can easily have a romantic dinner for two for under $100. The menu is a carnivore's delight: Beef includes the signature prime rib, a great steak au poivre, and a nod to cowboy machismo, the 22-ounce bone-in rib eye. The veal, pork chops, and rack of lamb are also topflight. A special treat is the exquisite chateaubriand for two, a steal at $75. However, seafood lovers shouldn't entirely skip Thoroughbreds, as the crab cakes and the shrimp and grits stack up to most any you'll find in the Carolinas.

The new darling of the steak-loving set is **Rioz Brazilian Steakhouse** (2920 Hollywood Dr., 843/839-0777, www.rioz.com, daily 4-10 P.M., $20-40). It's not cheap—the recommended 15-item meat sampler is about $35 pp—but then again, an experience this awesome shouldn't be cheap (a big plus is that kids under age 7 eat for free). The meats are fresh and vibrant, slow-cooked over a wood fire in the simple but succulent style typical of the gaucho *churrascaria* tradition. The service is widely considered to be the best in the area. But the biggest surprise may turn out to be the salad and seafood bar, which even has sushi.

There is no dearth of places to nosh at Barefoot Landing, but meat lovers (not to mention golfers) will probably enjoy **Greg Norman's Australian Grille** (4930 Kings Hwy. S., 843/361-0000, www.gregnormansaustraliangrille.com, lunch daily 11 A.M.-3 P.M., dinner daily 5-10 P.M., $20-30), which, despite the chain-sounding name, is the only restaurant of its kind. With the dark clubby ambience you'd expect at a place named for a golf pro, this is not necessarily where you want to take the kids. Instead, it's the place to enjoy a cocktail by the lake and a premium entrée like the lobster-crusted swordfish, the rack of lamb, or the prime rib.

For a less pricey but still very tasty experience, try **Liberty Tap Room and Grill** (7651 N. Kings Hwy., 843/839-4677, www.libertytaproom.com, daily 11 A.M.-11 P.M., $15-20). This regional chain not only boasts high-quality steaks and burgers in a casual atmosphere but has some good pizza and even seafood as well.

You wouldn't expect a place with the name **Carolina Roadhouse** (4617 N. Kings Hwy., 843/497-9911, Sun.-Thurs. 11 A.M.-10 P.M., Fri.-Sat. 11 A.M.-11 P.M., $10-28) to have excellent croissant appetizers, but that kind of twist is what makes this a cut above the usual steak-and-ribs joint. Virtually anything on the menu is very good, but since you're likely to be waiting for a table, you may as well go for the incredible ribs.

I normally shy away from mentioning national chain-type places because of the cheese factor, but I'll make an exception for Myrtle Beach, where you expect things to be a little cheesy. **Jimmy Buffett's Margaritaville** (1114 Celebrity Circle, 843/448-5455, www.margaritavillemyrtlebeach.com, Sun.-Thurs. 11 A.M.-10 P.M., Fri.-Sat. 11 A.M.-midnight, $13-22) at Broadway at the Beach is widely regarded as the best single location of the national chain. The signature Cheeseburger in Paradise is the obvious big hit. You get a lot of entertainment for your money as well, with balloon-twisting performers coming to your table and a bizarre whirling "hurricane" that acts up in the main dining area every now and then. As you'd expect, the margaritas are good, if expensive.

Many locals insist the better burger is at another Buffett-owned chain, the succinctly titled **Cheeseburger in Paradise** (7211 N. Kings Hwy., 843/497-3891, www.cheeseburgerinparadise.com, Sun.-Thurs. 11:30 A.M.-11 P.M., Fri.-Sat. 11:30 A.M.-midnight, $10-15), which offers a range of burgers on the menu with sweet potato chips on the side, all served up in a less flashy but still very boisterous atmosphere than the flagship restaurant.

CLASSIC SOUTHERN

If you've got a hankering for some spicy Cajun-creole food, go no farther than **The House of Blues** (4640 U.S. 17 S., 843/272-3000, www.hob.com, Mon.-Fri. 4-9 P.M., Sat. 8 A.M.-9 P.M., Sun. 9 A.M.-2 P.M. and 3-9 P.M., $10-25) at Barefoot Landing in North Myrtle Beach. With 17 similarly themed locations around North America, this particular venue deals in the same kind of retro Delta vibe, with specially commissioned folk art festooning the walls and live music cranking up at about 9 P.M. At your table, a gregarious server will walk you through the limited but intense menu, which includes such tasty bits as Buffalo Tenders (actually boneless chicken wings in a perfectly spicy sauce) and a couple of excellent jambalaya-type dishes. All portions are enormous and richly spiced. It's a loud, clanging room, so keep in mind that this is less a romantic experience than an exuberant earthy one.

A special experience at House of Blues is the weekly Gospel Brunch (9 A.M.-2 P.M. Sun., $20 adults, $10 ages 6-12), an opportunity not only to enjoy some tasty Southern-style brunch treats like cheese grits, jambalaya, and catfish tenders but to enjoy some really rather outstanding gospel entertainment at the same time. The Gospel Brunch is served in seatings, and reservations are recommended.

CONTINENTAL

In Myrtle Beach it can be difficult to find a good meal that's not fried or smothered or both. For a highbrow change of pace, try **The Library** (1212 N. Kings Hwy., 843/448-4527, www.thelibraryrestaurantsc.com, Mon.-Sat. 5-10 P.M., $20-50), which is hands-down the most romantic dining experience in Myrtle proper. It's not cheap, but then again, nothing about this place is pedestrian, from the very attentive European-style service to the savvy wine list and the signature dishes (many of them prepared tableside), like she-crab soup, Caesar salads, Steak Diane, and the ultimate splurge, steak and lobster.

Like art? Like food? Try the **Collector's Café** (7726 N. Kings Hwy., 843/449-9370, www.collectorscafeandgallery.com, $10-20), which, as the name implies, is a combined gallery and dining space. Don't be daunted by the strip mall setting—inside is a totally different ball game with a trendy open kitchen and plush, eclectic furniture awaiting you amid the original artwork. As for the menu, you may as well go for what's widely regarded as the best single dish, the scallop cakes. Make sure you save room for dessert.

ITALIAN

The best-regarded Italian place in Myrtle Beach—though it could just as easily go in the *Steaks* category, since that's its specialty—is **Angelo's** (2011 S. Kings Hwy., 843/626-2800, www.angelosteakandpasta.com, Sun.-Thurs. 4-8:30 P.M., Fri.-Sat. 4-9 P.M., $12-25). The signature dishes are intriguingly spiced cuts of steak (request beforehand if you don't want them seasoned), cooked medium and under for an exquisite tenderness. You can get spaghetti as a side with the steaks, or just go with the classic baked potato. Don't forget to check out the Italian buffet, including lasagna, Italian sausage, chicken cacciatore, ravioli, and, of course, pizza.

A particularly well-run franchise of a national chain, **Ultimate California Pizza** (2500 N. Kings Hwy., 843/626-8900, www.ultimatecaliforniapizza.com, daily 11 A.M.-11 P.M., $7-18) delivers the goods in Barefoot Landing in North Myrtle. They offer an almost bewildering variety of specialty pizzas, including a surf-and-turf pizza, one topped with filet mignon, and various interesting veggie styles. Many folks simply opt to build their own pie, however, with toppings such as apples and goat cheese and an incredibly diverse range of sauces.

WHAT'S A CALABASH?

In Myrtle Beach you'll no doubt see garish restaurant signs boasting of "Calabash Cooking" or a "Calabash Buffet." Named for a seaside shrimping and fishing village just over the border in North Carolina, Calabash cooking basically means fresh seafood that's fried in spiced corn meal soon after it's caught.

In usual practice, Calabash seafood is served in huge buffets, and to most people on the Strand the phrase really just refers to the sheer volume of food. Shrimp is the dominant motif, though flounder is big too. By all means enjoy Calabash cooking while you're on the Strand, but don't expect the catch to be fresh. Connoisseurs insist you need to go to Calabash, North Carolina, for that.

SEAFOOD

The grandest old Calabash seafood joint in town, **Original Benjamin's** (9593 N. Kings Hwy., 843/449-0821, daily 3:30-10 P.M., buffet $25 adults, $12 children) on the old Restaurant Row is one of the more unique dining experiences in Myrtle Beach. With themed rooms overlooking the Intracoastal Waterway, including the concisely named Bus Room—yes, it has an old school bus in it—you'll find yourself in the mood to devour copious amounts of fresh seafood at its humongous 170-item buffet line. That's not a misprint—170 items, including mounds of shrimp prepared in every style; all kinds of tuna, salmon, and catfish; a variety of crabmeat dishes; and nonseafood stuff like chicken and barbecue.

Closer to Broadway on the Beach, try **George's** (1401 29th Ave. N., 843/916-2278, www.captaingeorges.com, Mon.-Sat. 3-10 P.M., Sun. noon-9 P.M., buffet $31, $16 ages 5-12). Despite the usual kitschy nautical decor, this is the kind of place even locals will admit going to for the enormous seafood buffet, widely considered a cut above the norm.

With old reliables like crab cakes and sea scallops as well as signature house dishes like pecan-encrusted grouper and stuffed flounder, you can't go wrong at **The Sea Captain's House** (3002 N. Ocean Blvd., 843/448-8082, daily 6-10:30 A.M., 11:30 A.M.-2:30 P.M., and 5-10 P.M., $10-20), one of Myrtle Beach's better seafood restaurants. This opinion is widely held, however, so prepare to wait—often up to two hours. Luckily, you can sip a cocktail and gaze out over the Atlantic Ocean as you do so. Old hands will tell you it's not as good as back in the day, but it's still a cut above.

When you're at Ocean Drive Beach up in North Myrtle, check out another venerable old name, the **Duffy Street Seafood Shack** (202 Main St., 843/281-9840, www.duffyst.com, daily noon-10 P.M., $10). This is a humble unkempt roadside affair dealing in the kind of down-home treats Myrtle Beach seems to love ("pigskin" shrimp, fried pickles, and the like). Overall, it's a good place to get a tasty bite and soak in the flavor of this Cherry Grove neighborhood at the heart of the old shag culture.

Information and Services

The main visitors center for Myrtle Beach is the **Myrtle Beach Area Chamber of Commerce and Visitor Center** (1200 N. Oak St., 843/626-7444, www.visitmybeach.com, Mon.-Fri. 8:30 A.M.-5 P.M., Sat. 10 A.M.-2 P.M.). There's an **airport welcome center** (1180 Jetport Rd., 843/626-7444) as well, and a visitors center in North Myrtle Beach, the **North Myrtle Beach Chamber of Commerce and Convention & Visitors Bureau** (270 U.S. 17 N., 843/281-2662, www.northmyrtlebeachchamber.com).

The main health care facility in the Myrtle Beach area is **Grand Strand Regional Medical Center** (809 82nd Pkwy., 843/692-1000, www.grandstrandmed.com). Myrtle Beach is served by the **Myrtle Beach Police Department** (1101 N. Oak St., 843/918-1382, www.cityofmyrtlebeach.com). The separate municipality of North Myrtle Beach is served by the **North Myrtle Beach Police Department** (843/280-5555, www.nmb.us).

The newspaper of record for Myrtle Beach is *The Sun News* (www.myrtlebeachonline.com). For a look at the grittier side of Myrtle Beach music and nightlife, look for a copy of *The Weekly Surge* (www.weeklysurge.com).

In Myrtle Beach, you can choose between the main **U.S. Post Office** (505 N. Kings Hwy., 800/275-8777, Mon.-Fri. 8:30 A.M.-5 P.M., Sat. 9 A.M.-1 P.M.) or the other convenient location (820 67th Ave. N., 800/275-8777, Mon.-Fri. 9 A.M.-4:30 P.M., Sat. 11 A.M.-1 P.M.). In North Myrtle beach, try the main post office (621 6th Ave. S., 800/275-8777, Mon.-Fri. 8:30 A.M.-5 P.M., Sat. 9 A.M.-noon) or the other convenient location in Cherry Grove Beach (227 Sea Mountain Hwy., 800/275-8777, Mon.-Fri. 8:30 A.M.-5 P.M.).

Getting There and Around

GETTING THERE

The Myrtle Beach area is served by the fast-growing **Myrtle Beach International Airport** (MYR, 1100 Jetport Rd., 843/448-1589, www.flymyrtlebeach.com), which hosts Delta, Northwest, Southern Skyways, Spirit, U.S. Airways, and United.

Unusually for South Carolina, a state that is exceptionally well-served by the interstate highway system, the main route into the area is the smaller U.S. 17, which runs north-south, with a parallel business spur, from Georgetown up to the North Carolina border. The approach from the west is by U.S. 501, called Black Skimmer Trail as it approaches Myrtle Beach.

The local **Greyhound Bus terminal** (511 7th Ave. N., 843/231-2222) is in "downtown" Myrtle Beach.

GETTING AROUND

In practice, the Myrtle Beach municipalities blend and blur into each other in one long sprawl parallel to the main north-south route, U.S. 17. However, always keep this in mind: Just south of Murrells Inlet, U.S. 17 divides into two distinct portions. There's the U.S. 17 Bypass, which continues to the west of much of the coastal growth, and there's Business U.S. 17, also known as Kings Highway, the main drag along which most key attractions and places of interest are located.

The other key north-south route, Ocean Boulevard, runs along the beach. This is a two-lane road that can get pretty congested in the summer, especially when it's used for cruising by younger visitors or during one of the several motorcycle rallies throughout the year.

Thankfully, area planners have provided a great safety valve for some of this often horrendous traffic. Highway 31, the Carolina Bays Parkway, begins inland from Myrtle Beach at about 16th Avenue. This wide new highway roughly parallels the Intracoastal Waterway and takes you on a straight shot, with a 65 mph speed limit, all the way to Highway 22 (the Conway Bypass) or all the way to Highway 9 at Cherry Grove Beach, the farthest extent of North Myrtle Beach. The bottom line is that if time is of the essence, you should use Highway 31 whenever possible.

Rental Car, Taxi, and Bus

You will need a vehicle to make the most of this area. Rental cars are available at the airport. Rental options outside the airport include **Enterprise** (1377 U.S. 501, 843/626-4277; 3401 U.S. 17 S., 843/361-4410, www.enterprise.com), **Hertz** (851 Jason Blvd., 843/839-9530, www.hertz.com), and the unique **Rent-a-Wreck** (901 3rd Ave. S., 843/626-9393).

Taxi service on the Strand is plentiful but fairly expensive. Look in the local Yellow Pages for full listings; a couple of good services are **Yellow Cab** (917 Oak St., 843/448-5555) and **Beach Checker Cab** (843/272-6212) in North Myrtle.

The area is served by the **Coastal Rapid Public Transit Authority** (1418 3rd Ave., 843/248-7277), which runs several routes up and down the Strand. Ask at a visitors center or call for a schedule.

By Bicycle

Bicyclists in Myrtle Beach can take advantage of some completed segments of the South Carolina portion of the **East Coast Greenway** (www.greenway.org), which generally speaking is Ocean Boulevard. In Myrtle Beach there's a bike lane on North Ocean Boulevard from about 82nd Avenue North down to 29th Avenue North. You can actually ride Ocean Boulevard all the way from 82nd Avenue North down to the southern city limit, if you like. Inland, a portion of the Greenway is on Grissom Parkway, which takes you by Broadway at the Beach.

In North Myrtle Beach, from Sea Mountain Highway in Cherry Grove, you can bike Ocean Boulevard clear down to 46th Avenue South, with a detour from 28th to 33rd Avenues. A right on 46th Avenue South takes you to Barefoot Landing. And, of course, for a scenic ride, you can pedal on the beach itself for miles. But remember: Bicycling on the sidewalk is strictly prohibited.

As for bike rentals, try **Beach Bike Shop** (711 Broadway St., 843/448-5335, www.beachbikeshop.com). In North Myrtle, try **Wheel Fun Rentals** (91 S. Ocean Blvd., 843/280-7900, www.wheelfunrentals.com).

Points Inland

CONWAY

A nice day trip west of Myrtle Beach—and a nice change from that area's intense development—is to the charming town of Conway, just northwest of Myrtle Beach on U.S. 501 and the Waccamaw River. Founded in 1733 with the name Kingston, it originally marked the frontier of the colony. It was later renamed Conwayborough, soon shortened to Conway, in honor of local leader Robert Conway, and now serves as the seat of Horry County.

Conway's heyday was during Reconstruction, when it became a major trade center for timber products and naval stores from the interior. The railroad came through town in 1887 (later being extended to Myrtle Beach), and most remaining buildings date from this period or later. The most notable Conway native is perhaps an unexpected name: William Gibson, originator of the cyberpunk genre of science fiction, was born here in 1948.

Conway is small and easily explored. Make your first stop at the **Conway Visitors Center** (903 3rd Ave., 843/248-1700, www.cityofconway.com, Mon.-Fri. 9 A.M.-5 P.M.), where you can pick up maps. It also offers guided tours ($2 pp) that depart from City Hall (3rd Ave. and Main St.); call for a schedule. You can also visit the **Conway Chamber of Commerce** (203 Main St.) for maps and information.

Sights

Conway's chief attraction is the 850-foot **Riverwalk** (843/248-2273, www.conwayscchamber.com, daily dawn-dusk) along the blackwater Waccamaw River, a calming location with shops and restaurants nearby. Waterborne tours on the *Kingston Lady* leave from the Conway Marina at the end of the Riverwalk.

Another key stop is the **Horry County Museum** (428 Main St., 843/248-1542, www.horrycountymuseum.org, Tues.-Sat. 9 A.M.-4 P.M., free), which tells the story of this rather large South Carolina county from prehistory to the present. It holds an annual Quilt Gala in February, which features some great regional examples of the art.

Across from the campus of Coastal Carolina University is the circa-1972 Traveler's Chapel, a.k.a. **The Littlest Church in South Carolina** (U.S. 501 and Cox Ferry Rd.). At 12 by 24 feet, it seats no more than a dozen people. Weddings are held here throughout the year. Admission is free, but donations are accepted.

Accommodations

The best stay in town is at the four-star **Cypress Inn** (16 Elm St., 843/248-8199, www.acypressinn.com, $145-235), a beautiful and well-appointed 12-room B&B right on the Waccamaw River.

LEWIS OCEAN BAY HERITAGE PRESERVE

The humongous (over 9,000 acres) Lewis Ocean Bay Heritage Preserve (803/734-3886, www.dnr.sc.gov, daily dawn-dusk, free) is one of the more impressive phenomena in the Palmetto State, from a naturalist's viewpoint, made all the more special by its location a short drive from heavily developed Myrtle Beach. Managed by the state, it contains an amazing 23 Carolina bays, by far the largest concentration in South Carolina. These elliptical depressions, scattered throughout the Carolinas and all oriented in a northwest-southeast direction, are typified by a cypress-tupelo bog environment. The nearby Highway 31 is named the Carolina Bays Parkway in a nod to its neighbors. As if that weren't enough, the preserve boasts other unique aspects as well. It has the largest concentration of Venus flytraps in the state, and it is also said to be the only place in eastern South Carolina where black bears still live in the wild. Clemson University is conducting a study on their habits and so far has concluded that they roam back and forth between here and North Carolina. The birdwatching is extra-special too, with a good number of bald eagles and endangered red-cockaded woodpeckers in the area. Several miles of trails take you through a variety of habitats.

Keep in mind that despite its great natural beauty, the preserve is not pristine. As with most of Horry County, heavy logging and turpentine operations took place throughout the preserve's acreage during the 1800s and early 1900s. As with most South Carolina heritage preserves, hunting is allowed, and there are no facilities.

To get here from Myrtle Beach, take U.S. 501 north to Highway 90 and head east. After about seven miles, turn east on the unpaved International Drive across from the Wild Horse subdivision. After about 1.5 miles on International Drive, veer left onto Old Kingston Road. The preserve is shortly ahead on both sides of the road; park along the shoulder.

The Lower Grand Strand

Pawleys Island, Murrells Inlet, and the rest of the so-called Waccamaw Neck are the lower portion of the Grand Strand. While a certain amount of Myrtle Beach-style development is encroaching southward, this area is still far away in spirit and generally much more relaxed.

Tiny Pawleys Island (year-round population about 200) likes to call itself "America's first resort" because of its early role in the late 1700s as a place for planters to go with their families to escape the mosquito-infested rice and cotton fields; George Washington visited in 1791. It's still a vacation getaway and still has a certain elite understatement, an attitude the locals call "arrogantly shabby." Beach access is correspondingly more difficult than farther up the Strand near Myrtle Beach. While you can visit casually, most people who enjoy the

Brookgreen Gardens, America's largest outdoor sculpture collection

© SONJA WALLEN

famous Pawleys Island beaches do so from one of the many vacation rental properties. Shabby arrogance does have its upside, however—there is a ban on further commercial development in the community, allowing Pawleys to remain indefinitely slow and peaceful. The maximum speed limit throughout town is a suitably lazy 25 mph. For generations, Pawleys was famous for its cypress cottages, many on stilts. Sadly, 1989's Hurricane Hugo destroyed a great many of these iconic structures—27 out of 29 on the south end alone, most of which have been replaced by far less aesthetically pleasing homes.

Directly adjacent to Pawleys, Litchfield Beach offers similar low-key enjoyment along with a world-class golf resort. While several key attractions in the Grand Strand are technically in Murrells Inlet, that's more for post office convenience than anything else. Murrells Inlet is chiefly known for a single block of seafood restaurants on its eponymous waterway.

SIGHTS
◖ Brookgreen Gardens

One of the most unique—and unlikely—sights in the developed Grand Strand area is bucolic Brookgreen Gardens (1931 Brookgreen Dr., 843/235-6000, www.brookgreen. org, May-Mar. daily 9:30 A.M.-5 P.M., Apr. 9:30 A.M.-8 P.M., $14 adults, $7 ages 6-12, free under age 6), directly across U.S. 17 from Huntington Beach State Park. An eclectic compilation of sorts, Brookgreen combines scenic manicured gardens, copious amounts of outdoor sculpture by a host of artists, and a low-key but worthwhile nature center with live animals.

Once one of several massive contiguous plantations in the Pawleys Island area, the modern Brookgreen is a result of the charity and passion of Archer Milton Huntington and his wife, Anna Hyatt. Seeking to preserve the area's flora and fauna and celebrate American sculpture at the same time, the couple turned the entire place into a nonprofit in 1931. Quite the sculptor in her own right, Anna Huntington saw to it that Brookgreen's 9,000 acres would host by far the largest single collection of outdoor sculpture in the United States.

Designed and added onto over the past century, the sculpture gardens themselves are a sprawling collection of tastefully themed, colorfully planted gardens that are generally built around a key sculpture or two. As you're walking, don't forget to examine the various nooks, crannies, and corners inside and outside the walls where you'll find hundreds of smaller sculptures, generally along natural or mythological themes. The sculptures don't stop there—you'll see plenty of them out in the fields, overlooking lakes, and tucked into bushes all around the site. In all, there are over 1,200 works by more than 300 artists. While most sculptures tend toward a certain style—thick, robust, and often depicting some form of struggle—some are more whimsical and even downright charming, such as the one near the visitors center, which depicts several kids pledging allegiance to the flag. To learn more, visit the on-site **Carroll A. Campbell Jr. Center for American Sculpture,** which offers seminars and workshops throughout the year.

Botanists and green thumbs will find plenty to enjoy as well. At least 2,000 species of plants have been planted at Brookgreen, with something always guaranteed to be in bloom regardless of the season. A special treat is the stunning Oak Allee section, where some of the live oaks are 250 years old. One huge and ancient specimen, the Constitution Oak, has been designated a "living witness" to the signing of the U.S. Constitution.

On the other end of the grounds opposite the gardens is the **E. Craig Wall Jr. Lowcountry Nature Center,** which includes a small enclosed cypress swamp with a boardwalk, herons and egrets, and an absolutely delightful river otter exhibit, where you can see the playful critters swim and frolic. Other animals include alligators and several species of raptors. Almost all the animals have been treated for injuries that render them unfit to return to life in the wild.

To add an extra layer of enjoyment to your visit, you can explore this massive preserve much more deeply by taking one of several tours offered on Brookgreen's pontoon boat ($7 adults, $4 children on top of regular admission); check the website for a schedule.

◖ Huntington Beach State Park

Right across the street from Brookgreen is Huntington Beach State Park (16148 Ocean Hwy., 843/237-4440, www.southcarolinaparks.com, daily 6 A.M.-10 P.M., $5 adults, $3 ages 6-15, free under age 6), probably the best of South Carolina's state parks not built by the Civilian Conservation Corps. Once a part of the same vast parcel of land owned by Archer Huntington and his wife, Anna Hyatt, the state has leased it from the trustees of their estate since the 1960s.

You can tour the "castle" on the beach, Atalaya, former home of the Huntingtons and now the yearly site of the Atalaya Arts and Crafts Festival. This evocative Moorish-style National Historic Landmark is open to the public for free guided tours (Memorial Day-end of Sept. daily noon-1 P.M., Oct. 1-31 Tues.-Sat. noon-2 P.M., Sun.-Mon. noon-1 P.M.).

Today, a walk through the park is a delightful and convenient way to enjoy the Grand Strand's natural legacy. A great variety of birds use Huntington Beach as a migratory stopover. You can stroll three miles of beach, view birds and wildlife from several boardwalks into the marsh, hike several nature trails, and visit the well-done **Environmental Education Center** (843/235-8755, Tues.-Sun. 10 A.M.-5 P.M.), which features a saltwater touch tank and a baby alligator. In all, it's a great experience for the whole family, or a very romantic outing for a couple.

© JIM MOREKIS

Weston House in the Pawleys Island Historic District

Pawleys Island Historic District

Although many of the island's homes were leveled by Hurricane Hugo, the Pawleys Island Historic District (843/237-1698, www.townofpawleysisland.com) in the central portion of the island still has a dozen contributing structures, almost all on Myrtle Avenue. Among them are the **Weston House** (506 Myrtle Ave.), or Pelican Inn, and the **Ward House** (520 Myrtle Ave.), or Liberty Lodge. As you view the structures, many with their own historic markers, note the architecture. Because these were intended to be lived in May-November, they resemble open and airy Caribbean homes, with extensive porches and plenty of windows.

EVENTS

The highlight of the lower Grand Strand calendar is the annual **Atalaya Arts and Crafts Festival** (www.atalayafestival.com, $6 adults, free under age 16), which takes place on the grounds of Huntington Beach State Park each September. Like the park itself, the festival, now nearing its 40th year, is a philanthropic legacy of Archer Huntington and his wife, Anna Hyatt. There's music, food, and about 100 vendors who show their art and wares within the exotic Atalaya home. Admission to the park is free during the festival.

Also in September is the **Pawleys Island Festival of Music and Art** (www.pawleysmusic.com, prices vary), which happens outdoors, across U.S. 17 under the stars in Brookgreen Gardens, with a few performances at nearby Litchfield Plantation.

A main event in Murrells Inlet is the annual **Fourth of July Boat Parade** (843/651-0900, free), which celebrates American independence with a patriotically themed procession of all kinds of streamer- and flag-bedecked watercraft down the inlet. It begins at about 6 P.M. and ends, of course, with a big fireworks display.

Another big deal in Murrells Inlet is the annual **Blessing of the Inlet** (843/651-5099, www.belinumc.org), always held the first Saturday in May and sponsored by a local Methodist church. Enjoy food vendors, goods baked by local women, and a great family atmosphere.

SHOPPING

The shopping scene revolves around the famous Pawleys Island hammock, a beautiful and practical bit of local handiwork sold primarily at the **Hammock Shops Village** (10880 Ocean Hwy., 843/237-8448, Mon.-Sat. 10 A.M.-6 P.M., Sun. 1-5 P.M.). This is actually a collection of 25 shops and restaurants, the closest thing to a mall environment you'll find in the area.

To purchase a Pawleys Island hammock, go to **The Original Hammock Shop** (843/237-9122, www.thehammockshop.com), housed in a century-old cottage. Next door is the affiliated **Hammock Shop General Store,** which, as the name implies, sells a variety of other goods such as beachwear, books, and a notable style of local fudge. The actual hammocks are hand-crafted in the shed next door, the way they have been since 1889.

SPORTS AND RECREATION

Beaches

First, the good news: The beaches are pristine and beautiful. The bad news: Public access is very limited. Simply put, that means the best way to enjoy the beach is to rent one of the many private beach homes for a week or so. Although it's only a short distance from Myrtle Beach, the beaches at Pawleys and vicinity are infinitely more peaceful and easygoing.

Beach access with parking at Pawleys Island includes a fairly large lot at the south end of the island and parking areas off Atlantic Avenue at Hazard, 1st, Pearce, 2nd, and 3rd Streets, and Shell Road.

Kayaking and Canoeing

The Waccamaw River and associated inlets and creeks are peaceful and scenic places to kayak, with plenty of bird-watching opportunities to boot. For a two-hour guided tour of the area salt marsh, reserve a spot on the kayak trips sponsored by the **Environmental Education Center** (Huntington Beach State Park, 843/235-8755, office Tues.-Sun. 10 A.M.-5 P.M., $30 pp). Call for tour days and times. Or you can put in yourself at Oyster Landing, about one mile from the entrance to the state park.

Ecotours

The most popular and extensive dolphin tour in the area is the **Blue Wave Adventures Dolphin Watch** (843/651-3676, www.bluewaveadventures.com, $29 adults, $19 under age 13) on the waterfront in Murrells Inlet. The basic 90-minute tour leaves every day and takes you to the waters where the area pods, as well known as any local resident, tend to congregate. Call for tour times; morning tours are the best for finding dolphins.

Fishing

A good all-around charter operator in Murrells Inlet, **Capt. Dicks** (4123 Business U.S. 17, 843/651-3676, www.captdicks.com, prices vary), runs a variety of trips, from deep-sea sportfishing to more casual inshore adventures. Dicks also offers nonfishing trips, such as a dolphin tours and a popular marsh ecotour. It's in the same building as Spuds restaurant.

Golf

Home to some of the best links in the Carolinas, the lower part of the Grand Strand recently organized its courses under the umbrella moniker **Waccamaw Golf Trail** (www.waccamawgolftrail.com), chiefly for marketing purposes. No matter, the courses are still as superb as ever, if generally pricier than their counterparts up the coast.

The best course, hands down, in the area, and one of the best in the country, is the **Caledonia Golf and Fish Club** (369 Caledonia Dr., 843/237-3675, www.fishclub.com, $195). While the course itself is almost ridiculously young—it opened in 1995—this masterpiece is built, as so many area courses are, on the grounds of a former rice plantation. The clubhouse, in fact, dates from before the Civil War. Besides its signature 18th hole, other hallmarks of Caledonia are its copious amount of very old live oaks and its refusal to allow homes or condos to be built on the grounds. Packages are available (800/449-4005, www.myrtlebeachcondorentals.com). Affiliated with Caledonia is the fine **True Blue Golf Club** (900 Blue Stem Dr., 843/235-0900, www.fishclub.com, $100), considered perhaps the most challenging single course on the Strand.

Another excellent Pawleys course, and one with a significantly longer pedigree, is the **Litchfield Country Club** (U.S. 17 and Magnolia Dr., 843/237-3411, www.litchcc.com, $60), one of the Grand Strand's oldest courses and the first in Pawleys Island. The facilities are self-consciously dated—this is a country club, after all—setting it apart from the flashier, newer courses sprouting like mushrooms farther up the Strand. It's a deceptive course that's short on yards but heavy on doglegs.

The Jack Nicklaus-designed **Pawleys Plantation Golf and Country Club** (70 Tanglewood Dr., 843/237-6100, www.pawleysplantation.com, $150) has set a tough example for the last 20 years. Beautiful but challenging, it has a Jekyll-and-Hyde nature. The front nine is a traditional layout, while the back nine melts into the marsh.

ACCOMMODATIONS
Under $150
Similarly named but definitely not to be confused with Litchfield Plantation is the nearby **Litchfield Beach and Golf Resort** (14276 Ocean Hwy., 866/538-0187, www.litchfieldbeach.com, $100-170). In typical Grand Strand fashion, this property delivers a lot of service for a surprisingly low price. Also typical for the area, it offers a wide range of lodging choices, from a basic room at the Seaside Inn on the low end to four-bedroom villas ($230, still a great deal). Though not all units are right on the beach, a regular free shuttle takes you to the sand pretty much whenever you want. There are also lots of water activities right on the premises, including a ubiquitous "lazy river" tube course.

$150-300
The premier B&B-style lodging on the entire Grand Strand is ◖ **Litchfield Plantation** (Kings River Rd., 843/237-9121, www.litchfieldplantation.com, $230-275) on Pawleys Island, built, as you've probably come to expect by now, on an old plantation. There is a host of lodging choices, all of them absolutely splendid. The Plantation House has four sumptuous suites, all impeccably decorated. The humbly named Guest House—actually an old mansion—has six bedrooms, and the entire second floor is an executive suite. Lastly, the newer outparcel Villas contain an assortment

of two- and three-bedroom suites. Amenities include a complimentary full plantation breakfast each morning and a three-story beach club for use only by guests. If you visit in the winter, you can get a room for as little as $150, a heck of a deal regardless of the temperature outside.

Vacation Rentals
Many who enjoy the Pawleys area do so using a vacation rental as a home base rather than a traditional hotel or B&B. **Pawleys Island Realty** (88 N. Causeway Rd., 800/937-7352, www.pawleysislandrealty.com) can hook you up.

Camping
For great camping in this area, go no farther than **Huntington Beach State Park** (16148 Ocean Hwy., 843/237-4440, www.southcarolinaparks.com, daily 6 A.M.-10 P.M., $5 adults, $3 ages 6-15, free under age 6). The beach is beautiful, there are trails and an education center, and the bird-watching is known as some of the best on the East Coast. While there are 131 RV-suitable sites ($23-28), tenters should go to one of the six walk-in tent sites ($17-19).

FOOD
Breakfast and Brunch
The high-end strip mall setting isn't the most romantic, but by broad consensus the best breakfast on the entire Strand is at **Applewood House of Pancakes** (14361 Ocean Hwy., 843/979-1022, daily 6 A.M.-2 P.M., $5-10) in Pawleys. Eggs Benedict, specialty omelets, crepes, waffles, and pancakes abound in this roomy, unpretentious dining room. Do it; you won't regret it.

Seafood
The Pawleys-Litchfield-Murrells Inlet area has some good seafood places, although the long lines during high season at some of the better-known, more touristy places are not necessarily a sign of quality. A visit in the fall or winter

brings a culinary treat to help take the chill off: fresh local oysters. Do keep in mind that many restaurants keep substantially shorter hours in the winter, and some close completely.

Murrells Inlet has several good places clustered together along the marsh on U.S. 17. The best is **Lee's Inlet Kitchen** (4460 Business U.S. 17, 843/651-2881, www.leesinletkitchen. com, Mar.-Nov. Mon.-Sat. 4:30-10 P.M., $20-40), which is the only original Murrells Inlet joint still in the original family—in this case the Lee family, who started the place in the mid-1940s. The seafood is simply but delectably prepared (your choice of fried or broiled), with particular pride taken in its freshness. Their sole drawback is that they close down December-February.

Along similar lines and almost as recommendable is **Flo's Place Restaurant** (3797 Business U.S. 17, 843/651-7222, www. flosplace.com, daily 11 A.M.-10 P.M., $15-25). Flo is sadly no longer with us, but her place still eschews schlock for a more humble, down-home feel. Everything is fresh, hot, and tasty, from the fried green tomatoes to the crab cakes and the alligator nuggets—yes, it's real alligator meat; they like to say it tastes like a cross between chicken and veal. But the signature dish is the legendary Dunkin' Pot—a big kettle filled with oysters, clams, shrimp, potatoes, sausage, and seasonal shellfish. As if that weren't enough, it's topped with snow crab legs. Do save room for some fried pickles.

On the other end of the spectrum style-wise is **Divine Fish House** (3993 Business U.S. 17, 843/651-5800, www.divinefishhouse.com, daily 5-10 P.M., $20-33), which offers more adventurous high-end cuisine like the fine San Antonio Salmon (smothered with pepper-jack

cheese and bacon) and the Asian-flavored Banana Leaf Mangrove Grouper.

Just down the road at Pawleys is **Hanser House** (14360 Ocean Hwy., 843/235-3021, www.hanserhouse.com, daily 4-10 P.M., $19), which offers succulent seafood dishes like its signature crabmeat-stuffed flounder or king crab legs, but also offers some crackerjack steaks. Check out their frequent oyster roasts October-February.

Coffee, Tea, and Sweets

A favorite is **Kudzu Bakery** (221 Willbrook Blvd., 843/235-8560, www.kudzubakery.com, Mon.-Fri. 9 A.M.-6 P.M., Sat. 9 A.M.-3 P.M.), recognizable from its popular original spot in Georgetown and similarly renowned for delectable fresh-baked goodies.

INFORMATION AND SERVICES

On Pawleys Island is the **Georgetown County Visitors Bureau** (95-A Centermarsh Lane, 843/235-6595, www.visitgeorgetowncountysc. com). The **Myrtle Beach Area Chamber of Commerce** (3401 U.S. 17, 843/651-1010, www. visitmybeach.com) and the new **Waccamaw Community Hospital** (4070 U.S. 17 Bypass, 843/652-1000, www.georgetownhospital-system.org) are in Murrells Inlet. Pawleys Island is served by the **Pawleys Island Police Department** (321 Myrtle Ave., 843/237-3008, www.townofpawleysisland.com).

Pawleys Island has a small newspaper, the *Coastal Observer* (www.coastalobserver.com). Pawleys Island has a **U.S. Post Office** (10993 Ocean Hwy., 800/275-8777, Mon.-Fri. 8 A.M.-4:30 P.M., Sat. 10 A.M.-noon), as does Murrells Inlet (654 Bellamy Ave., 800/275-8777, Mon.-Fri. 8:30 A.M.-5 P.M., Sat. 9 A.M.-noon).

Georgetown and Vicinity

Think of Georgetown as Beaufort's lesser-known cousin. Like Beaufort, it's an hour away from Charleston, except to the north rather than to the south. Like Beaufort, it boasts a tidy historic downtown that can be walked from end to end in an afternoon. And like Beaufort, it was once a major center of Lowcountry plantation culture.

However, Georgetown gets significantly less attention and less traffic. Unlike Beaufort, no movies are shot, and no rambling Southern memoirs were penned here. Certainly the fact that the entrance to town is dominated by the sprawling ominous-looking Georgetown Steel mill on one side of the road and the massive smelly International Paper plant on the other has something to do with it. Make no mistake; industry is a way of life here. An important seaport for most of its history, Georgetown today boasts South Carolina's second busiest port after Charleston. But when you take a quick turn to the east and go down to the waterfront, you'll see the charm of old Georgetown: bright, attractive, historical homes, cute shops and cafés, and the peaceful Sampit River flowing by.

There are several enjoyable and educational places a short way north on U.S. 17. Chief among them are Hobcaw Barony, former playground of the rich turned environmental education center, and Hampton Plantation, a well-preserved look back into antebellum elegance and rice-culture history. Indeed, the coastal stretch from Georgetown down to the Charleston suburb of Mt. Pleasant is an inexplicably underrated microcosm of the Lowcountry that's easy to travel, relatively rustic, yet close enough to "civilization" that you never really have to leave your comfort zone.

One particularly delightful aspect is the fact that the massive Francis Marion National Forest is your constant companion on the west side of U.S. 17—helping to keep at bay much of the egregious overdevelopment that is taking place elsewhere on the South Carolina coast. The forest also provides plenty of hiking, biking, and bird-watching opportunities.

HISTORY

The third-oldest city in South Carolina, after Charleston and Beaufort, Georgetown was founded in 1729 on a four- by eight-block grid, most of which still exists today, complete with original street names.

Georgetown's influence was acute during the American Revolution, with the father-son team of Palmetto State signers of the Declaration of Independence Thomas Lynch and Thomas Lynch Jr. both hailing from here. The Revolutionary War hero Francis Marion, the "Swamp Fox," was born in nearby Berkeley County and conducted operations in and around the area during the entire war, including an unsuccessful assault on British forces holding Georgetown.

The biggest boom was still ahead for Georgetown. While Charleston-area plantations get most of the attention, the truth is that by 1840 about 150 rice plantations on the Sampit and Little Pee Dee Rivers were producing half of the entire national output of the staple crop. Indeed, Georgetown held fast to rice even as most Southern planters switched to growing cotton after the invention of the cotton gin.

After the Civil War, the collapse of the slave-based economy (at its height, 90 percent of Georgetown's population was slaves) meant the relative collapse of the rice economy as well. Although the plantations stayed in operation, their output was much smaller, and the coming of the boll weevil infestation in the early 1900s merely brought it to a merciful end.

In 1905 Bernard Baruch—native South Carolinian, Wall Street mover and shaker, and

THE SPANISH AT WINYAH BAY

The Georgetown area is best known for its Anglophile tendencies in history, character, and architecture. But before the English came the Spanish.

Beautiful Winyah Bay outside Georgetown–estuary of the Sampit, Pee Dee, Black, and Waccamaw Rivers–was the site of one of the first landfalls by Europeans in the New World. It happened in 1526 when six Spanish ships, commanded by Lucas Vázquez de Ayllón, came to establish a colony in the area.

The wealthy heir to a sugar-planting fortune on Hispaniola in the Caribbean, Ayllón was also a master of PR. On a previous scouting trip, he had captured an Indian and brought him back to Spain. Upon hearing the captive's proud descriptions of his homeland, King Charles V promptly gave Ayllón permission to settle the area, just as Ayllón had hoped. The king was pretty crafty himself; he insisted that Ayllón mount the expedition at his own expense.

Upon arrival with his 500 colonists, Ayllón's reluctant Indian passengers–including his only adviser to presidents—came to town, purchasing Hobcaw Barony, a former plantation. It became his winter residence and hunting ground, and his legacy of conservation lives on there today in an education center on the site.

interpreter, the same man he'd brought before the king–vanished into the maritime forest, never to be found. Even worse for the Spanish, one of Ayllón's ships, the *Capitana*, sank in Winyah Bay with most of the expedition's supplies. It remains there to this day, though no one knows quite where it is or what is left of it.

Ayllón would finally get his colony, though not in South Carolina. Finding the local soil too acidic for crops and the local Native Americans too scarce in number to provide dependable slave labor, he decamped and headed down the coast to the area of St. Catherine's Sound in modern-day Georgia. His settlement there, San Miguel de Gualdape, lasted only a few months until falling victim to disease, poor nutrition, and Indian attack. But it was indeed the first European colony in what would become the United States–preceding the Spanish settlement at St. Augustine, Florida, by nearly 40 years and the first English colony at Jamestown, Virginia, by almost a century.

adviser to presidents—came to town, purchasing Hobcaw Barony, a former plantation. It became his winter residence and hunting ground, and his legacy of conservation lives on there today in an education center on the site.

The Depression was particularly hard on Georgetown, with virtually the entire city being unemployed at one point. But in 1936, the opening of a massive paper mill turned things around, with economic effects that you can see (and olfactory effects that you can smell, unfortunately) to this day.

Today, Georgetown is a quiet place where most people either make their living working at the port, the steel mill, or the paper plant, with a good smattering of tourism-related businesses in the historic district. On the national level it's perhaps best known for being the hometown of comedian Chris Rock; although he moved away long ago, many members of his family continue to live here, and he usually pays a visit at Christmas.

SIGHTS
Kaminski House

The city of Georgetown owns and operates the historic Kaminski House (1003 Front St., 843/546-7706, www.cityofgeorgetownsc. com, Mon.-Sat. 9 A.M.-5 P.M., Sun. 1-4 P.M., $7 adults, $3 ages 6-12, free under age 6). Built in 1769, it was home to several city mayors, including Harold Kaminski, who ran the city from 1931 to 1935. "Stately" pretty much describes the elegant exterior of this two-story masterpiece, but the real goods are inside. It's furnished with a particularly exquisite and copious selection of 18th- and 19th-century antiques. The grounds are beautiful as well, overlooking the Sampit River and lined with Spanish moss-covered oaks.

The only way to see the inside of the house is to take the free 45-minute guided tour. Fortunately, they're quite frequent, generally departing every hour on the hour

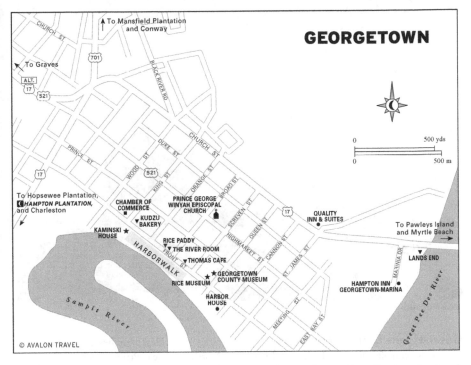

Monday-Saturday 10 A.M.-4 P.M. and Sunday 1-4 P.M.; call ahead to confirm tour times.

Rice Museum

The succinctly named Rice Museum (633 Front St., 843/546-7423, www.ricemuseum.org, Mon.-Sat. 10 A.M.-4:30 P.M., $7 adults, $3 ages 6-21, free under age 6) is just that: A look back at the all-important staple crop and its massive effects on Georgetown, which at one point accounted for half of the country's rice production.

There are actually two parts of the museum: The Old Market building, often simply called "The Town Clock" because of its 1842 timepiece, hosts the bulk of the archival information on the impact of rice growing on the region's history and economy; the adjacent Kaminski Hardware building includes a 17-minute video on the rice industry, a good Gullah-Geechee cultural exhibit, and a gift shop. However, its

main claim to fame is the collection of regional maritime history, including the remains of the oldest colonial boat in North America, the 50-foot *Brown's Ferry Vessel*, built in 1710.

Several key exhibits in the Rice Museum trace the fundamental but generally reluctant role in the rice industry of African Americans, almost all of whom were slaves and who comprised nearly 90 percent of the local population during the height of the rice industry. You'll learn the story of Joseph Rainey, the first African American elected to the U.S. House of Representatives, who once worked in the fields around Georgetown. You'll learn about Miss Ruby Forsythe, who spent her life teaching African American children in a one-room school on Pawleys Island.

Most visitors to the Rice Museum take a one-hour guided tour, included in the price of admission.

© JIM MOREKIS

Rice Museum

Georgetown County Museum

For a more complete look at all aspects of local history, check out the Georgetown County Museum (632 Prince St., 843/545-7020, Tues.-Fri. 10 A.M.-5 P.M., Sat. 10 A.M.-3 P.M., $4 adults, $2 ages 6-18, free under age 6). The highlight is a recently discovered letter written by Francis Marion.

Prince George Winyah Episcopal Church

It has seen better days—the British partially burned it during the Revolution—but Prince George Winyah Episcopal Church (301 Broad St., 843/546-4358, www.pgwinyah.org, Mon.-Fri. 11:30 A.M.-4:30 P.M., services Sun. 8 A.M., 9 A.M., and 11 A.M.) is still a fine example of the Anglican tradition of the Lowcountry rice culture. First built in 1750 out of ballast stones (the parish itself dates from substantially earlier, 1721), the sanctuary features classic box pews, expert stained glass, and ornate woodwork on the inside. The bell tower dates from 1824.

One of the oldest churches in continuous use in North America, Prince George is certainly worth preserving. The parish has formed its own nonprofit group, the Preservation Trust for Historic Prince George Winyah Church (843/546-4358), to raise funds and direct conservation efforts.

Hopsewee Plantation

Beautiful in an understated way, Hopsewee Plantation (494 Hopsewee Rd., 843/546-7891, www.hopsewee.com, Feb.-Nov. Tues.-Fri. 10 A.M.-4 P.M., Sat. noon-4 P.M., Dec.-Jan. by appointment only, $17.50 adults, $10.50 ages 12-17, $7.50 ages 5-11) on the Santee River 12 miles south of Georgetown was the birthplace of Thomas Lynch Jr., one of South Carolina's signers of the Declaration of Independence. Some key archaeological work is going on at the former slave village on this old indigo plantation; you can visit two of the original slave cabins on the tour.

THE SWAMP FOX AND THE COMING OF GUERRILLA WARFARE

I have it from good authority, that this great soldier, at his birth, was not larger than a New England lobster, and might easily enough have been put into a quart pot.

Peter Horry,
who fought with Francis Marion

Short, bowlegged, and moody, Francis Marion was as far away from the template of the dashing war hero as his tactics were from the storybook exploits of military literature. The father of modern guerrilla warfare was born an unimpressively small and sickly baby, the youngest of seven, somewhere in Berkeley County, South Carolina, in 1732 to hardworking French Huguenot parents. Soon his family would move near Georgetown on the coast, and the teenage Marion became enamored with the sea. While his infatuation with maritime life lasted exactly one voyage—a whale rammed and sank his ship—a taste for adventure remained.

During the French and Indian War, Marion fought local Cherokees, and revisionist historians would later revile the enthusiasm he showed in this venture. But Marion's own words show a more conflicted character, as shown by his reaction to an order to burn Cherokees out of their homes.

Some of our men seemed to enjoy this cruel work, laughing very heartily at the curling flames, as they mounted loud crackling over the tops of the huts. But to me it appeared a shocking sight. *Poor creatures!* thought I, we surely need not grudge you such miserable habitations.

While the irregular tactics Marion learned fighting the Cherokee would come in handy during the Revolution, his first experience in that conflict was in more textbook engagements, such as the defenses of Fort Moultrie and Fort Sullivan and the siege of Savannah. But with the fall of Charleston in 1780, a vengeful Marion and his ragged band of volunteer fighters—who, unusually for the time, included African Americans—vanished into the bogs of the Pee Dee and took up a different way of warfare: ambush and retreat, harass and vanish. In a foreshadowing of the revolutionary movements of the 20th century, "Marion's Men" provisioned themselves with food and supplies from a sympathetic local populace, offering receipts for reimbursement after the war.

Astride small agile mounts called Marsh Tackies, descendants of horses originally left by the Spanish, the Patriots rode where bigger British cavalry horses balked. Marion's nocturnal cunning and his superior intelligence network frustrated the British army and their Loyalist supporters to no end, leading to his nickname, "The Swamp Fox."

British Colonel Banastre Tarleton, himself known as "The Butcher" for atrocities on civilians, was dispatched to neutralize Marion. The savage cat-and-mouse game between the two formed the basis for the storyline of Mel Gibson's 2000 film *The Patriot* (Gibson's character was reportedly a composite of Marion and several other South Carolina irregulars). Filmed entirely in South Carolina—including at Middleton Plantation, Cypress Gardens, and Historic Brattonsville—*The Patriot* is far from an exact chronicle, but it does accurately portray the nature of the war in the Southern theater, in which quarter was rarely asked or given, and little distinction was made between combatant and civilian.

While certainly the most famous, the Swamp Fox was merely first among equals in a veritable menagerie of hit-and-run fighters. Thomas Sumter, a Virginian by birth, became known as "The Carolina Gamecock" for his ferocity on the battlefield. Andrew Pickens, "The Wizard Owl," and his militiamen played a key role in the Battle of Cowpens in the Upstate.

After the war, Marion served in elected office, married, and settled down at his Pine Bluff Plantation, now submerged under the lake that bears his name. He died in 1795 at the age of 63, peaceful at last.

While not as grand as many other Lowcountry plantation homes, the 1740 main house is a masterpiece of colonial architecture, and all the more impressive because it's very nearly original, with the black cypress exterior largely intact. The focus here is on preservation, not restoration.

The home and its surrounding plantation were owned by the wealthy planter Thomas Lynch, one of South Carolina's original delegates to the First Continental Congress. While deliberating in Philadelphia in 1776, Lynch suffered a severe stroke. His son, Thomas Jr., asked for leave from the South Carolina militia in order to tend to his ailing father. The request was denied, but the state legislature intervened and named the 26-year-old a delegate to the Continental Congress so he could join his father. And that's how the Lynches became the only father-son team of signers of the Declaration of Independence—in spirit,

anyway: There's an empty signature line on the original Declaration between South Carolina's Edward Rutledge and the younger Lynch; the elder Lynch, who would die shortly afterward, was physically unable to sign his name.

Unusually, this home remains in private hands, and as such it has a more lived-in feel than other house museums of its type. There's a fairly active calendar of events throughout the year, including sweetgrass basket-weaving classes in the basement. Check the website for info on specific events.

◖ Hampton Plantation

Tucked away three miles off U.S. 17 on the South Santee River is Hampton Plantation State Historic Site (1950 Rutledge Rd., 843/546-9361, www.southcarolinaparks. com, grounds open daily, call for hours, free, house tours $7.50 adults, $3.50 ages 6-15). This Georgian gem, one of the grandest of the

Hampton Plantation

© JIM MOREKIS

antebellum Lowcountry homes, hosted George Washington in 1791. It was also the home of South Carolina poet laureate Archibald Rutledge, who sold it to the state in 1971. Because it's now a state-run project, admission fees are significantly lower than at most of the private plantation homes in the area.

Hampton's pedigree is a virtual who's who of great South Carolina family names. In addition to the Rutledges, the Pinckneys and the Horries also called it home at one time or another.

The imposing antebellum main house, circa 1735, is magnificent both inside and out, with some of the rooms remaining unfurnished to better explain the architecture. The grounds are gorgeous as well, overflowing with live oaks, azaleas, and camellias. If you want to skip the house tour, visiting the grounds is free. A two-mile nature trail takes you around one of the original rice fields on Wambaw Creek.

St. James-Santee Episcopal Church

This redbrick church doesn't look that old, but the sanctuary of St. James-Santee Episcopal Church (Old Georgetown Rd., 843/887-4386), south of Georgetown near Hampton Plantation State Historic Site, dates from before the Revolutionary War. While it suffered damage from Union troops during and after the Civil War, much of it is intact.

A registered National Historic Landmark and known simply as "the brick church" to differentiate it from a church in nearby McClellanville that more often hosts the present congregation, it dates from 1768, but the St. James-Santee parish it serves was actually the second in the colony after St. Michael's in Charleston. The parish was notable for incorporating large numbers of French Huguenots.

The interior is nearly as Spartan as the exterior, featuring the rare sight of old-fashioned family pews. While the brick was imported from Britain, the columns are made of cypress. Look for original plasterwork on the ceiling.

Today, only one official service is held each year in the old brick church, during Easter.

McClellanville

The tiny and almost unbearably cute little fishing village of McClellanville is nestled among the woods of Francis Marion National Forest and is known mostly for the annual **Lowcountry Shrimp Festival and Blessing of the Fleet** (http://lowcountryshrimpfestival.com) held on the waterfront in early May. This is the place to go for any kind of delectable fresh shrimp dish you might want, from fried shrimp to shrimp kebabs and shrimp tacos. The event culminates with the colorful and touching Blessing of the Fleet ceremony.

Hobcaw Barony

Once a plantation, then a winter home for a Wall Street investor, and now an environmental education center, Hobcaw Barony (22 Hobcaw Rd., 843/546-4623, www.hobcawbarony.org, hours and prices vary) is one of the more unusual stories of the Lowcountry. Its name comes from a Native American word meaning "between the waters," an allusion to its location on the Waccamaw Neck, the beginnings of the Grand Strand itself. By 1718 the surrounding land comprised various rice plantations, among South Carolina's earliest, which stayed in operation through the end of the 1800s.

Hobcaw entered its modern period when 11 of the former plantations were purchased en masse in 1905 by Wall Street investor Bernard Baruch, a South Carolina native who wanted a winter residence to escape the brutal Manhattan winters. Presidents and prime ministers came to hunt and relax on its nearly 18,000 acres.

Fifty years later, Baruch died, and his progressive-minded daughter Belle took over, immediately wanting to open the grounds for university and scientific research. Still privately owned by the Belle W. Baruch Foundation, much of Hobcaw Barony is open only to researchers, but the **Hobcaw Barony Discovery Center** (843/546-4623, www.hobcawbarony. org, Mon.-Fri. 9 A.M.-5 P.M., free) has various exhibits on local history and culture, including Native American artifacts and a modest but fun aquarium with a touch tank.

To experience the rest of Hobcaw Barony, you must take one of the various themed guided tours (call for days and times). The basic Hobcaw tour ($20) takes you on a three-hour van ride all around the grounds, including the main Hobcaw House, historic stables, and the old slave quarters, with an emphasis on the natural as well as human history of the area. Other special tours include Birding on the Barony ($30), Christmas in the Quarters ($20), and a catch-and-release fly-fishing tour ($250) of local waters.

Georgetown Lighthouse

While you can't access the state-owned Georgetown Lighthouse, you can indeed take a trip to the beach on North Island, where the lighthouse stands. The 1811 structure, repaired after heavy damage in the Civil War, is still an active beacon, now entirely automated.

North Island was part of lands bequeathed to the state by former Boston Red Sox owner Tom Yawkey. North Island is now part of a wildlife preserve bearing Yawkey's name. In 2001, the Georgetown Lighthouse was added to the preserve, and it is also on the National Register of Historic Places.

Tours and Cruises

One of the most sought-after tour tickets in the Georgetown area is for the annual **Plantation Home Tour** (843/545-8291). Sponsored by the Episcopal Church Women of Prince George Winyah Parish, this event, generally happening the first week in April, brings visitors onto many local private antebellum estates that are not open to the public at any other time. Each ticket is for either the Friday or Saturday tour,

both of which feature a different set of homes. Tickets include tea at the Winyah Indigo Society Hall each afternoon.

For a standard downtown tour, get on one of the blue-and-white trams of **Swamp Fox Historic District Tours** (1001 Front St., 843/527-6469, $10 pp), which leave daily on the hour starting at 10 A.M. near the Harborwalk.

The best walking tour of Georgetown is **Miss Nell's Tours** (843/546-3975, Tues. and Thurs. 10:30 A.M. and 2:30 P.M., other times by appointment, $7-24 depending on tour length chosen). Leaving from the Harborwalk Bookstore (723 Front St.), Miss Nell, who's been doing this for over 20 years, takes you on a delightful trek through Georgetown's charming downtown waterfront.

Water dominates life in this region, and that may just be the best way to enjoy it. One of the more interesting local waterborne tours is on board the *Jolly Rover* and *Carolina Rover* (735 Front St., 843/546-8822, www.rovertours. com, Mon.-Sat., times and prices vary). The *Jolly Rover* is an honest-to-goodness tall ship that takes you on a two-hour tour of beautiful Winyah Bay and the Intracoastal Waterway, all with a crew in period dress. The *Carolina Rover* takes you on a three-hour ecotour to nearby North Island, site of the historic Georgetown Lighthouse. You can't tour the lighthouse itself, but you can get pretty darn close to it on this tour. The always-entertaining **Cap'n Sandy's Tours** (343 Ida Dr., 843/527-4106) also takes you to North Island in the shadow of the Lighthouse; call for times and rates.

For a more intense maritime ecotourism experience, contact **Black River Outdoors Center and Expeditions** (21 Garden Ave., 843/546-4840, www.blackriveroutdoors.com). Their stock-in-trade is a nice half-day kayak tour ($55 adults, $35 under age 13), generally including creeks in and around Huntington Beach and through the fascinating matrix of blackwater and cypress swamps that once

BROAD STREET TO WALL STREET: THE STORY OF BERNARD BARUCH

He became one of the country's most influential men and a world-famous adviser to presidents during both world wars, but Bernard Baruch never strayed far in spirit from his South Carolina home.

Born to German-Jewish parents in the town of Camden, near Columbia, Baruch was born a mere five years after the end of the Civil War. Ironically, his father emigrated from Prussia to avoid the draft, but soon after arriving in the United States, he found himself a surgeon on Robert E. Lee's staff.

Educated in New York City, Baruch gained a love of finance and a taste for the high life. By age 30 he had become so wealthy playing the market that he was able to buy a seat on the New York Stock Exchange. It was during this phase of his life that he purchased the 18,000-acre Hobcaw Barony near Georgetown, a conglomeration of several former rice plantations that became his hunting retreat, a hallowed place of solitude where no phones were allowed.

Baruch's prowess in the realm of high finance led him to a post as adviser to President Woodrow Wilson; perhaps influencing the selection was the whopping $50,000 contribution Baruch gave to Wilson's 1914 campaign, an enormous sum for that time. Required to divest his funds and give up his stock-exchange seat, Baruch turned his aggressive financier's mind to a larger playing field. A sort of economic czar for the Wilson administration, he would play a key role in mobilizing American industry for the war effort, turning what had been a largely agrarian rural society into a modern manufacturing juggernaut.

Under President Franklin D. Roosevelt, Baruch was a key member of the New Deal's National Recovery Administration and favored a centralized (some said heavy-handed) approach to organizing the national economy. While this served him well during the New Deal and World War II, his often idealistic approach—which envisioned a key role of the United States as an enforcer of nuclear nonproliferation—fell out of favor with the Truman administration's realpolitik. Still, Baruch would leave his mark on the postwar era as well: He was the first to coin the phrase *Cold War*, in a speech in 1947.

Indeed, Baruch was always a colorful and succinct communicator, no doubt a legacy of his Southern boyhood. He is said to have originated the witticism "If all you have is a hammer, everything looks like a nail." Other great one-liners of his include "Millions saw the apple fall, but only Newton asked why," and "Old age is always 15 years older than I am."

Baruch died in New York City in June 1965, but he spent all that May down in South Carolina at Hobcaw Barony. By that time his daughter Belle had purchased most of Hobcaw and would eventually deed it to a foundation in her name, administered by the University of South Carolina and Clemson University.

Baruch's boyhood home in Camden is no more, but it is commemorated with a marker on Broad Street. You can also enjoy the beauty and tranquility of **Hobcaw Barony** (22 Hobcaw Rd., 843/546-4623, www.hobcawbarony. org, hours and prices vary) for yourself.

hosted the rice kingdom of Georgetown and vicinity. They also offer a harbor tour ($35 pp).

For a much simpler, less nature-oriented water tour, try **Cap'n Rod's Lowcountry Tours** (843/477-0287, www.lowcountrytours.com). Rod's pontoon boat is on the Harborwalk just behind the Rice Museum. A three-hour Plantation River Tour (Mon.-Sat. 10 A.M.) costs about $25 adults, $20 children.

ENTERTAINMENT AND EVENTS

The **Winyah Bay Heritage Festival** (632 Prince St., 843/833-9919, www.winyahbay. org, free) happens each January at various venues and benefits the local historical society. The focus is on wooden decoys and waterfowl paintings, similar to Charleston's well-known Southeast Wildlife Exposition.

Each October brings the delightful **Wooden**

Boat Show (843/545-0015, www.woodenboatshow.com, free) to the waterfront, a 20-year-old celebration of, you guessed it, wooden boats. These aren't toys but the real thing—sleek, classic, and beautiful in the water. There are kid's activities, canoe-making demonstrations, a boat contest, and the highlight, a boatbuilding challenge involving two teams working to build a skiff in four hours.

SHOPPING

As you might expect, the bulk of shopping opportunities in Georgetown are down on the waterfront, chiefly at **The Shoppes on Front Street** (717-A Front St., 843/527-0066), the umbrella name for an association of downtown merchants. Highlights include **Harborwalk Books** (723 Front St., 843/546-8212, www.harborwalkbooks.com) and the children's boutique **Doodlebugs** (721 Front St., 843/546-6858).

SPORTS AND RECREATION
Kayaking and Canoeing

Kayakers and canoeists will find a lot to do in the Georgetown area, the confluence of five rivers and the Atlantic Ocean.

A good trip for more advanced paddlers is to go out **Winyah Bay** to undeveloped North Island. With advance permission from the state's Department of Natural Resources (803/734-3888), you can camp here. Any paddling in Winyah Bay is pleasant, whether you camp or not.

Another long trip is on the nine-mile blackwater **Wambaw Creek Wilderness Canoe Trail** in the Francis Marion National Forest, which takes you through some beautiful cypress and tupelo habitats. Launch sites are at the Wambaw Creek Boat Ramp and a bridge landing. Other good trips in the national forest are on the Santee River and Echaw Creek.

For rentals and guided tours, contact **Nature Adventures Outfitters** (800/673-0679), which runs daylong paddles (about $85 pp), and **Black**

River Outdoors Center and Expeditions (21 Garden Ave., 843/546-4840, www.blackriveroutdoors.com), which runs a good half-day tour ($55 adults, $35 under age 13). For those who want to explore the intricate matrix of creeks and tidal canals that made up the Georgetown rice plantation empire, a guided tour is essential.

Occasional kayak ecotours leave from the **Hobcaw Barony Discovery Center** (843/546-4623, www.hobcawbarony.org, Mon.-Fri. 9 A.M.-5 P.M., $50) under the auspices of the **North Inlet Winyah Bay National Estuarine Research Reserve** (843/546-6219, www.northinlet.sc.edu).

Fishing

Inshore saltwater fishing is big here, mostly for red drum and sea trout. For the full-on Georgetown fishing experience, contact **Delta Guide Service** (843/546-3645, www.deltaguideservice.com), which charges about $350 per day for a fishing charter along the coast.

Hiking

The **Francis Marion National Forest** (www.fs.fed.us) hosts a number of great hiking opportunities, chief among them the Swamp Fox passage of the **Palmetto Trail** (www.palmettoconservation.org). This 47-mile route winds through longleaf pine forests, cypress swamps, bottomland hardwood swamps, and various bogs, much of the way along an old logging rail bed. The main entrance to the trail is near Steed Creek Road off U.S. 17; the entrance is clearly marked on the west side of the highway.

Another way to access the Swamp Fox passage is at **Buck Hall Recreation Area** (843/887-3257) on the Intracoastal Waterway. This actually marks the trailhead of the Awendaw Connector of that part of the Palmetto Trail, a more maritime environment. Another trailhead from which to explore Francis Marion hiking trails is farther down U.S. 17 at the **Sewee Visitor**

Center (5821 U.S. 17, 843/928-3368, www.fws. gov/seweecenter, Tues.-Sat. 9 A.M.-5 P.M.).

Golf

The closest really good links to Georgetown are the courses of the **Waccamaw Golf Trail** (www.waccamawgolftrail.com), a short drive north on U.S. 17. The best public course close to Georgetown is the **Wedgefield Plantation Golf Club** (129 Clubhouse Lane, 843/546-8587, www.wedgefield.com, $69), on the grounds of an old rice plantation on the Black River about four miles west of town. A famous local ghost story revolves around Wedgefield; allegedly the ghost of a British soldier, beheaded with a single slash from one of Francis Marion's men, still wanders the grounds.

ACCOMMODATIONS
Under $150

Close to the historic district is **Quality Inn & Suites** (210 Church St., 843/546-5656, www. qualityinn.com, $90-140), which has an outdoor pool and an included breakfast. On the north side of town on U.S. 17 you'll find the **Hampton Inn Georgetown-Marina** (420 Marina Dr., 843/545-5000, www.hamptoninn. com, $140-170), which also offers a pool and complimentary breakfast.

$150-300

By far the most impressive lodging near Georgetown—and indeed among the most impressive in the Southeast—is ◖ **Mansfield Plantation** (1776 Mansfield Rd., 843/546-6961, www.mansfieldplantation.com, $150-200), a bona fide antebellum estate dating from a 1718 king's grant. It is so evocative and so authentic that Mel Gibson shot part of his film *The Patriot* here, and renovation was recently completed on a historic slave chapel and cabin. As is typical of the Georgetown area, you will find the prices almost ridiculously low for this unique experience on this historic 1,000-acre

tract, with gardens, trails, and free use of bicycles. Pets can even stay for an extra $20 per day. As for you, you can stay in one of nine guest rooms situated in three guesthouses on the grounds, each within easy walking distance of the public areas in the main house, which include a 16-seat dining room.

With the closing of the longtime favorite B&B, the Dupre House, it's left to another B&B, the **Harbor House** (15 Cannon St., 843/546-6532, www.harborhousebb.com, $159-189), to carry on the tradition. Its four riverfront suites are perhaps slightly more modernized than you'd expect in this Georgian home, with eight fireplaces and heart-pine floors. But step into either the living room or the dining room, where the sumptuous breakfasts are served, and it's like 1850 again.

FOOD

Don't be fooled by Georgetown's small size—there's often a wait for tables at the better restaurants.

Breakfast and Brunch

The *Southern Living*-recommended **Thomas Cafe** (703 Front St., 843/546-7776, www.thomascafe. net, Mon.-Fri. 7 A.M.-2 P.M., Sat. 7 A.M.-1 P.M., $5-9) offers awesome omelets and pancakes in addition to more Lowcountry-flavored lunch dishes like crab-cake sandwiches and fried green tomatoes.

Classic Southern

Georgetown's best-known fine-dining establishment is **The Rice Paddy** (732 Front St., 843/546-2021, www.ricepaddyrestaurant.com, lunch Mon.-Sat. 11:30 A.M.-2 P.M., dinner Mon.-Sat. 6-10 P.M., $20-30), with the name implying not an Asian menu but rather a nod to the town's Lowcountry culture. Set inside a former bank building, the interior is a bit more modern than you might expect. The seafood is strong, but they do a mean veal scaloppine and rack of lamb as well. Reservations are strongly recommended.

Coffee, Tea, and Sweets

A perennial favorite is ◖ **Kudzu Bakery** (120

King St., 843/546-1847, Mon.-Fri. 9 A.M.-5:30 P.M., Sat. 9 A.M.-2 P.M.), renowned for its fresh-baked goodies such as delectable breakfast muffins, velvety chocolate cakes, and seasonal pies with fresh ingredients like strawberries, peaches, and pecans.

Seafood

Find the best shrimp and grits in town at **The River Room** (801 Front St., 843/527-4110, www.riverroomgeorgetown.com, Mon.-Sat. 11:30 A.M.-2:30 P.M. and 5-10 P.M., $15-25), which combines a gourmet attitude in the kitchen with a casual attitude on the floor. However, dishes like the herb-encrusted grouper or the signature crab cakes taste like fine dining all the way. Reservations are not accepted, and dress is casual. Literally right on the waterfront, the dining room in this former hardware store extends 50 feet over the Sampit River, adjacent to a public dock where many diners arrive by boat. There's even a large aquarium inside to complete the atmosphere.

Over at the Georgetown Marina, with great views of the river, is **Lands End** (444 Marina Dr., 843/527-1376, Mon.-Fri. 11 A.M.-2:30 P.M. and 5-9:30 P.M., Sat. 5-9:30 P.M., Sun. 11 A.M.-2:30 P.M., $15-25), which serves good Southern-style seafood and prime rib in a relaxing atmosphere.

INFORMATION AND SERVICES

In the historic waterfront area, you'll find the **Georgetown County Chamber of Commerce and Visitor Center** (531 Front St., 843/546-8436, www.georgetownchamber.com). **Georgetown Memorial Hospital** (606 Black River Rd., 843/527-7000, www.georgetownhospitalsystem.org) is the main medical center in the area; this 131-bed institution is in the middle of a proposed expansion and relocation. If you need law enforcement help, call the **Georgetown Police** (2222 Highmarket St., 843/545-4300, www.cityofgeorgetownsc.com). In emergencies call 911.

The newspaper of record in Georgetown is the **Georgetown Times** (www.gtowntimes.com). An unofficial visitors' guide to the town is **Harborwalk** (www.theharborwalk.com), a monthly newsletter geared toward visitors. For your postal needs, visit Georgetown's main **U.S. Post Office** (1101 Charlotte St., 800/275-8777, Mon.-Fri. 9 A.M.-5 P.M., Sat. 10 A.M.-noon).

GETTING THERE AND AROUND

Georgetown is at the extreme southern tip of the Grand Strand, accessible by U.S. 17 from the east and south and U.S. 521 (called Highmarket St. in town) from the west. Very centrally located for a tour of the coast, it's about an hour north of Charleston and slightly less than an hour from Myrtle Beach.

Though there's no public transportation to speak of in Georgetown, its small size makes touring fairly simple. Metered parking is available downtown.

www.moon.com

DESTINATIONS | ACTIVITIES | BLOGS | MAPS | BOOKS

MOON.COM is ready to help plan your next trip! Filled with fresh trip ideas and strategies, author interviews, informative travel blogs, a detailed map library, and descriptions of all the Moon guidebooks, Moon.com is all you need to get out and explore the world—or even places in your own backyard. While at Moon.com, sign up for our monthly e-newsletter for updates on new releases, travel tips, and expert advice from our on-the-go Moon authors. As always, when you travel with Moon, expect an experience that is uncommon and truly unique.

KEEP UP WITH MOON ON FACEBOOK AND TWITTER
JOIN THE MOON PHOTO GROUP ON FLICKR

MAP SYMBOLS

Symbol	Name	Symbol	Name	Symbol	Name	Symbol	Name
≈≈≈	Expressway	🅒	Highlight	✗	Airfield	⚑	Golf Course
——	Primary Road	○	City/Town	✗	Airport	🅿	Parking Area
——	Secondary Road	◉	State Capital	▲	Mountain	⬟	Archaeological Site
- - - -	Unpaved Road	⊛	National Capital	✛	Unique Natural Feature	⬧	Church
- - - -	Trail	★	Point of Interest			▮	Gas Station
··········	Ferry	•	Accommodation	🦅	Waterfall	⬭	Glacier
←←←	Railroad	▾	Restaurant/Bar	▲	Park		Mangrove
≈≈≈	Pedestrian Walkway	▪	Other Location	🎋	Trailhead		Reef
⊞⊞⊞	Stairs	⋀	Campground	⛷	Skiing Area		Swamp

CONVERSION TABLES

°C = (°F - 32) / 1.8
°F = (°C x 1.8) + 32
1 inch = 2.54 centimeters (cm)
1 foot = 0.304 meters (m)
1 yard = 0.914 meters
1 mile = 1.6093 kilometers (km)
1 km = 0.6214 miles
1 fathom = 1.8288 m
1 chain = 20.1168 m
1 furlong = 201.168 m
1 acre = 0.4047 hectares
1 sq km = 100 hectares
1 sq mile = 2.59 square km
1 ounce = 28.35 grams
1 pound = 0.4536 kilograms
1 short ton = 0.90718 metric ton
1 short ton = 2,000 pounds
1 long ton = 1.016 metric tons
1 long ton = 2,240 pounds
1 metric ton = 1,000 kilograms
1 quart = 0.94635 liters
1 US gallon = 3.7854 liters
1 Imperial gallon = 4.5459 liters
1 nautical mile = 1.852 km

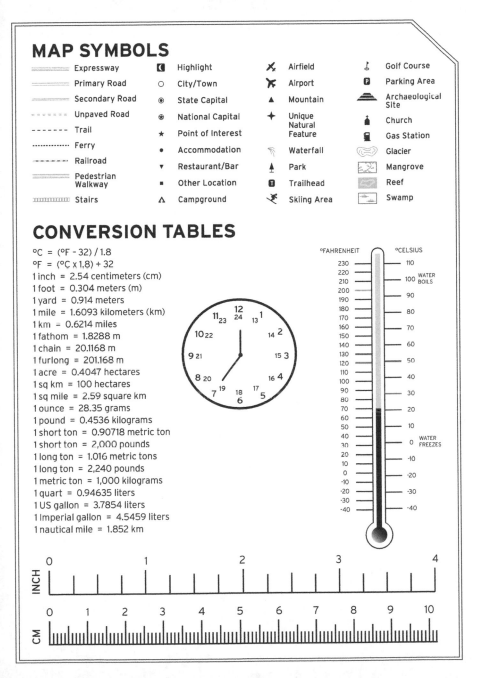

MOON SPOTLIGHT MYRTLE BEACH
Avalon Travel
a member of the Perseus Books Group
1700 Fourth Street
Berkeley, CA 94710, USA
www.moon.com

Editor and Series Manager: Kathryn Ettinger
Copy Editor: Christopher Church
Graphics Coordinator: Tabitha Lahr
Production Coordinator: Tabitha Lahr
Cover Designer: Kathryn Osgood
Map Editor: Kat Bennett
Cartographers: June Thammasnong, Chris Henrick

ISBN-13: 978-1-61238-496-2

Text © 2013 by Jim Morekis.
Maps © 2013 by Avalon Travel.
All rights reserved.

Title page photo: Brookgreen Gardens © Andrew
Kazmierski/www.123rf.com

Printed in Canada by Friesens

All recommendations, including those for sights,
activities, hotels, restaurants, and shops, are based
on each author's individual judgment. We do not
accept payment for inclusion in our travel guides,
and our authors don't accept free goods or services
in exchange for positive coverage.

Although every effort was made to ensure that
the information was correct at the time of going
to press, the author and publisher do not assume
and hereby disclaim any liability to any party for any
loss or damage caused by errors, omissions, or any
potential travel disruption due to labor or financial
difficulty, whether such errors or omissions result
from negligence, accident, or any other cause.

ABOUT THE AUTHOR

Jim Morekis

Jim Morekis grew up just a stone's throw from South Carolina – in Savannah, Georgia – and he's used to Charlestonians regarding his hometown as a wayward little sibling. As a young boy who loved history, Jim was fascinated with the home of the Swamp Fox and its key role in the Revolution and the Civil War. As he got older, he discovered a more important truth about the Palmetto State: Few places in America provide such a wealth of experience in such a small package.

Jim's favorite South Carolina pastimes include relaxing on Edisto Island, eating shrimp and grits in Charleston, waterfall-spotting in the Upstate, playing miniature golf at Myrtle Beach, enjoying a cold brew in Columbia's Five Points, walking through old cemeteries, and listening to Dizzy Gillespie while in the jazzman's hometown of Cheraw. He is also learning to appreciate stock car racing. Jim works as a journalist and travel writer, and in his spare time enjoys going shopping with his wife, Sonja, and daughters Sophia and Alex on Charleston's King Street.

Jim chronicles Southern life and times and the history of the old Morekis family dairy at www.morekisdairy.com.

CPSIA information can be obtained at www.ICGtesting.com
Printed in the USA
LVOW04s0254050914

402422LV00009B/23/P